Cookshire's Pine Hill Farm
The land, the people.

Winston C. Fraser

© 2019 Winston Fraser Consulting Inc.

1225 rue Bellevue
Saint-Lazare, QC J7T 2L9
438-969-2510
wcfraser@sympatico.ca

All rights reserved. No part of this book may be adapted, reproduced or transmitted in any form or by any means, electronic, mechanical, photocopying, recording, microrecording, or otherwise, without the written permission of Winston Fraser Consulting Inc.

Layout and production: Jim Fraser

Front cover photos:
    Top: Hibbert Newton Binney, "Typical Wabanaki Encampment of the Late 1700s" (koasek-abenaki.com)
    Middle: Original Pine Hill farmhouse, the first framed house in Eaton Township, ca. 1898 (Fraser family archives)
    Bottom: Winter view of Pine Hill Farm from railway, ca. 1965 (author)

Dedication page photo: Fraser family archives

Back cover photos:
    Top: Pine Hill Farm mailbox (author)
    Author's photo: Fraser family archives

Printed and bound in Canada by:

Katari Imaging
282 Elgin St.
Ottawa, ON K2P 1M3
613-233-1999
www.katariimaging.com

ISBN: 978-0-9950842-9-2

Contents

Dedication 4

Foreword 5

Acknowledgements 6

Preface 9

Chapter 1   In the Beginning: First Nations Peoples 13

Chapter 2   Orsamus & Margaret: From America for Land 27

Chapter 3   James & Abigail: From Quebec City for Love 47

Chapter 4   Charles & Lilla: Bricks and Mortar 59

Chapter 5   Donald & Alice: Indoor Plumbing and Outdoor Ponds 73

Chapter 6   Malcolm & Doreen: Modern Methods and Community Care 99

Chapter 7   The Railways: The Boom and the Bust 121

Chapter 8   The Sugar Bush: How Sweet it Was! 137

Chapter 9   Cookshire Fair : Farmers' Wares and Ferris Wheels 157

Chapter 10   The Eaton River: From Salmon to Sawmills 175

Chapter 11   The Town of Cookshire: Proximity and Partnership 193

Chapter 12   Memories, Miracles, Mysteries and Musings 215

Epilogue 239

Bibliography 241

Dedication

This book is lovingly dedicated to my older brother, Malcolm Fraser (affectionately known to his siblings as "Moose" and to his friends as "Mac"), who farmed this land for more than 50 years and whose interest in researching and preserving family history provided me with much valuable material for this book. Unfortunately, because he is now incapacitated, he cannot appreciate what he helped to produce. However, many others will be afforded that opportunity, and for that I say "Thank you, Moose!"

Foreword

Author's note: *I am very honoured that Bernard Hodge, a long-time family friend and fellow descendant of Eaton Township pioneers, has agreed to write the Foreword for this book.*

The greater Fraser family has lived in Cookshire for several generations dating back to the late 1700s. During that time they have contributed to the welfare of the town and its inhabitants in a very positive way. Notable among their involvement have been the summer Cookshire Fair and the fall/winter Seed Fair. Indeed, Malcolm Fraser was very actively involved in all aspects of these Fairs – from being a director of the Compton County Agricultural Society to being president for many years.

The Fraser and Hodge families have a history of working together over the years. Before the days of artificial insemination, I remember Mr. Fraser (Donald) leading a cow a distance of 5 km up to my dad's farm to be bred. In that way, we helped ensure the production of milk for the Fraser family.

The original Fraser property extended from above the farmhouse and farm buildings, down across the Eaton River to the meadowland below. I believe that the land under the river also belonged to the original owners. The hay from the meadows had to be hauled by horse and wagon across the river and up the steep hill to the barns. It made haying a long and difficult process.

This is the story not only of Pine Hill Farm but also of the earliest inhabitants of the land. It traces the history from the presence of the Abenaki First Nations to the arrival in 1797 of American Orsamus Bailey, the first "white" incumbent, to its cultivation by several succeeding generations of the Fraser family.

I would highly recommend this book to anyone interested in the early history of this part of the Eastern Townships. It is an excellent read.

– Bernard Hodge, retired high school principal, Cookshire, Que.

Acknowledgements

I wish to acknowledge the invaluable assistance of my siblings and my children for their recollections of Pine Hill Farm. In addition, I want to recognize the contributions of other family members and friends who so kindly shared their memories and/or photographs. The list is long and I apologize in advance to anyone who may have been inadvertently omitted. To all of the following I extend my sincere thanks:

Alan Marcus, Almon Pope, Andrea Fraser, Barbara Ward, Bea Nelson, Ben Hodge, Carl Jackson, Carol Rand, Catherine Lavoie (Bibliothèque et Archives nationales du Québec), Charles C. Fraser, Charles W. K. Fraser, Chris Standish, David Fraser, Diane Fraser Keet, Doreen Tryon Fraser, Dorothy Shelton Dionne, Elaine Fraser, Elizabeth Fraser, Éric Graillon, Frasier Bellam, Janice Fraser, Jim Fraser, Jim MacKinnon, Jim Robinson, (the late) Jim Shaughnessy, Jody Robinson (Eastern Townships Resource Centre), John "Jack" Fraser, John Thévenot, June Fraser Patterson, Karen Fraser Jackson, Karine Savary (La Société d'histoire de Sherbrooke), Malcolm "Mac" Fraser, Marc Nault, Marilyn Fraser Reed, (the late) Marina Fraser Tracy, Muriel French Fitzsimmons, Neil Burns, Robert Burns, Rodger Heatherington, Ron Planche, Sally Aldinger, Sharon Moore, Sharron Hodge Rothney, Steve Fraser, Theda Jackson Lowry, Tim Fraser, Warren Fraser.

I would be remiss not to mention the valuable information contained in the daily diaries and accounting journals kept by my late grandmother, Lilla Joyce Fraser, and by my late mother, Alice Hood Fraser. These records that have been preserved by my siblings were of enormous help in providing a window into our family's everyday happenings over more than 100 years. Their detailed analysis by my brother Warren allowed me to select from them the most pertinent information. I also want to thank artist James Harvey for the excellent sketches that he created to illustrate situations for which no photos were available, and my son-in-law, Greg Beck, for his professional photo retouching. Finally, a special word of appreciation to my brother Jim for his expert proofreading, layout and production services.

I have attempted to accurately credit the sources for all photographs and other images contained in this book. In the case of any missing credits, it can be assumed that the source is the Fraser family archives.

Magazine article featuring Alice Fraser's diary (*Farm Woman News*, June 1985)

Pine Hill Farm historical document storage box (photo by author)

Preface

Aerial view of Pine Hill Farm, with the main farm west of the river outlined (sigale.ca)

This is the story of a farm like no other. Officially designated as "Range 8 parts of Lots 9 and 10" of Eaton Township, Cookshire's Pine Hill Farm is unique in so many ways: its geographic features, the great variety of crops grown, the Noah's ark collection of animals raised, and the unusual woodpecker-like shape of the property. The farm takes its name from the ten giant white pine trees that lined the road and the sloping terrain. Among its physical features are hilly rocky fields, flat fertile meadowlands, a rich conifer forest, a maple sugar bush, spring-fed ponds stocked with fish, a babbling brook and a river that runs right through the property. The panoply of planted products includes an extensive variety of vegetables, fruits and berries, ranging from hops to horseradish to haricots. In terms of livestock, in addition to the expected bovine, equine, porcine and ovine species, there have been fur-bearing vixen and flocks of feathered fowl, including turkeys, geese, ducks and pigeons.

It is also the story of the five generations of the Bailey-Fraser family, who farmed this land over a period that spanned four centuries. During that time, they have tilled the fields, pampered the animals and toiled night and day to eke out a hard but honourable living on this land. This book documents their tenacity in times of trial, their creativity in a climate of challenge, and their faithfulness in the face of failure. And it reveals some heretofore untold stories of near-disasters, mysterious disappearances and family feuds.

Pine Hill Farm house and mailbox, ca. 1970 (photo by author)

However, this book is something more than all that. My original intent was simply to write about my ancestors and the land they farmed. Doing so would effectively complete my trilogy of family history publications. *OHIXIHO: The Biography of Charles Clark Fraser* was published in 2016, and *Dew Drop Inn: Lasting Memories of a Cookshire Landmark* the following year. But my conscience was suddenly pricked when I recently came across two very similar statements in the Sunday service bulletins of local Anglican and United churches:

> We acknowledge the traditional territory upon which we gather. For many thousands of years the Abenakis and the Wabenaki Confederacy

nations have sought to walk gently on this land. They offered assistance to the first European travellers to this territory and shared their knowledge for survival in what was at times a harsh climate. We seek a new relationship with the Original Peoples of this land, one based in honour and deep respect. (deaneryofstfrancis.com)

For thousands of years, First Nations peoples have walked on this land; their relationship with the land is at the centre of their lives and spirituality. We are gathered on the traditional territory of the Abenaki and acknowledge their stewardship of this land throughout the ages. (plymouthtrinitychurch.org)

Similarly, the home page of nearby Champlain College's website declares:

The Champlain Lennoxville community respectfully acknowledges that the beautiful land on which we study, live and learn is the traditional and unceded territory of the Abenaki people and the Wabenaki Confederacy. (crc-lennox.qc.ca)

These very clear acknowledgements of an historical truth represent one of the results of Canada's Truth and Reconciliation Commission whose "Calls to Action" included:

Repudiate concepts used to justify European sovereignty over Indigenous lands and peoples such as the Doctrine of Discovery and *terra nullius*. (nctr.ca)

My interest in the history of Canada's First Nations peoples began in high school, where I won a public speaking contest on the topic "The North American Indian." Some decades later I had the opportunity to visit Waskaganish, a Cree community in the James Bay region, where my eldest daughter, Andrea, worked for 10 years as a school guidance counsellor. During that same period, as a Board member of the Canadian Bible Society, I was exposed to the Mohawk First Nations community with respect to the translation of several books of the Bible into their native language. But the real watershed awareness moment for me was when I encountered the declarations mentioned above. Therefore, I find it incumbent upon me to not limit the scope of this book to the history of my own ancestors, but rather to broaden it to include the important history of the First Nations peoples who preceded them on the land I call home. May this recognition also serve to enhance the reader's appreciation of this tome.

Please note that certain spelling, grammar or syntax errors in quoted texts have been corrected in order to improve clarity and enhance readability.

Chapter 1
In the Beginning: First Nations Peoples

"Typical Wabanaki Encampment of the Late 1700s" (watercolour by Hibbert Newton Binney, koasek-abenaki.com)

This story begins long before my great-great-grandfather settled on the land that came to be known as Pine Hill Farm. In fact, it begins many hundreds – even thousands – of years earlier. This reality provides a new perspective on history, as so well expressed by the Bartlett, N.H., town's website:

> We current residents and our ancestors are still "newbies" in the broader historical perspective. Other folks lived here long before us. Paleoindians were living in this area about 11,300 years ago (9,300 BCE). Small groups of families migrated seasonally to hunt and gather various floras, gradually moving about along the waterways and primitive trails. Their way of life was successful, and so the population grew. There is debate about how these early people got here, but many Native Americans believe that their ancient ancestors originated on this continent . . . (bartletthistory.org)

Following in the footsteps of the Paleoindian tribes several thousand years later were the Abenaki First Nations peoples. To understand who they were and where they came from, I have excerpted information from various sources knowledgeable of that period of our prehistory.

Origin and Identity

An understanding of the Abenaki peoples' origin and identity may be obtained from three Internet sources directly related to their history:

> The Waban-Aki (Abenaki), "People of the Rising Sun," originated from New England, where some of their descendants still live. Beginning in 1675, a number of Abenaki took refuge in the St. Lawrence Valley because of their numerous conflicts with the American colonies. They settled in the Quebec City region before locating along the Saint-François and Bécancour rivers. The Abenaki subsisted partly on agriculture, but hunting and fishing occupied a very important place in their way of life. ("Aboriginal Peoples: Fact and Fiction," autochtones.gouv.qc.ca)

Map of First Nations of Northeastern North America (smore.com)

> The clothes worn by the Abenaki varied according to the season. In the hot, humid summer, the men wore breechcloths tucked over a belt that hung to mid-thigh at the back. The breechcloths were often accompanied by leather leggings kept in place with strips of cloth like garters to protect their legs. The leggings tapered towards the ankle and the outside was decorated with a fringe or beadwork. Moccasins were made with a long tongue and a high collar that could be folded up or down. In

Abenaki couple in the 18th century (Wikipedia.com)

the wet and snowy winters, snowshoes were also worn. The Abenaki women wore deerskin wraparound skirts or dresses and also wore leggings. In the winter, cloaks made from buckskin or other animal skins were worn by both men and women. The Abenaki also wore highly distinctive, embellished pointed or peaked hoods made from birchbark or leather that covered the shoulder decorated with feathers or tufts of animal hair at the point. . . The Abenaki Native Americans built canoes made from the bark of the birch trees over a wooden frame. These lightweight birchbark canoes were broad enough to float in shallow streams, strong enough to shoot dangerous rapids, and light enough for one man to easily carry a canoe on his back. (warpaths2peacepipes.com)

Among the First Nations of northeastern North America, several nations formed alliances, such as the Iroquois, Delaware and Cree confederacies. In the middle of the 18th century, the First Nations of Maine and the

Maritimes founded the Wabanaki Confederacy in the context of a peace treaty with the Mohawks, who were their old enemy. (forum.autochtones.ca; translated from French by author)

Territory

The Abenakis occupied a vast territory that extended from the Atlantic coast to the St. Lawrence River, from the Richelieu to the St. John River valley. They were thus in the current provinces of Quebec and New Brunswick and the states of Maine, New Hampshire, Vermont, Massachusetts, Connecticut, Rhode Island as well as the coastlines of New Jersey, Delaware, Virginia, Maryland and North Carolina. The arrival of the Europeans at the beginning of the 17th century changed all that. As a result of frequent bloody wars against the English colonists and numerous epidemics of all sorts and the constant impingement on their traditional territory, the Abenakis were pushed to the northern limit of their territory situated in New France . . . However the Quebec Abenakis never lost contact with their New England brothers. . . . The Abenakis are made up of a mosaic of different tribes of similar cultures and languages. (Pierre Paré, "La Toponymie de Abénaquis," toponymie.gouv.qc.ca; translated from French by author)

Prehistory

The table below summarizes the presence of Amerindian peoples (in what is now southern Quebec) up until the historic period.

Chronology of Amerindian Peopling up to the Historic Period

Timeframe	Events
ca. 10,000 BC	Amerindians coming from the south and west enter present-day Québec. Called Paleo-Indians, they specialize in caribou hunting. They occupy the regions of the Eastern Townships, Rimouski and the Gaspé Peninsula.
ca. 4000 BC	The Amerindian occupation intensifies. These nomadic populations live by hunting, fishing and gathering. The use of a wide variety of natural resources is reflected in an increased number of tools made of flaked or ground stone. This period is referred to as the Archaic.
ca. 1500 BC	The population grows and lifestyles change, particularly in the St. Lawrence Valley. The introduction of pottery and farming, adopted from societies living to the south characterizes this period, known as the Woodland.
ca. 1000 AD	The Iroquoian populations of southern Québec adopt a more sedentary lifestyle, farming and living in longhouses in villages with populations of up to 2 000 or more. These people are the St. Lawrence Iroquoians, whom Jacques Cartier encounters along the shores of the St. Lawrence River in 1534. Algonquian groups, on the other hand, continue to live off the fruits of the land, by fishing, hunting and gathering.
16th Century	The St. Lawrence Iroquoians are at war with the Algonquians and the Hurons. By 1608, they have disappeared from the St. Lawrence Valley. Their disappearance is a topic of heated debate among archaeologists and historians.

(archeoquebec.com)

In the Beginning

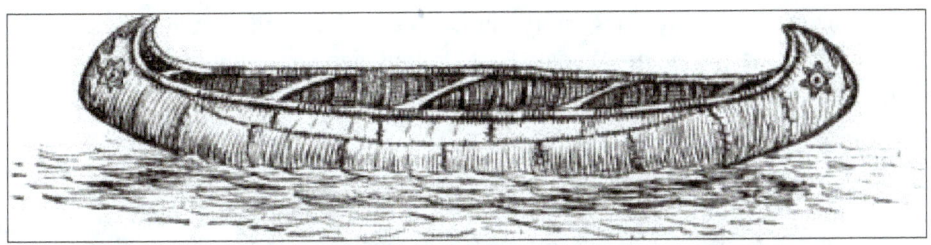

Abenaki birchbark canoe (www warpaths2peacepipes.com)

The Storyteller Paleoindians (bartletthistory.org)

It is impossible to accurately explain in a few short paragraphs the relationships that existed between the indigenous peoples and the European settlers. The two short extracts below illustrate some aspects of that relationship:

> While there were atrocities committed by both the native populace and early settlers, many early stories point to the basic peaceful nature of the native inhabitants, particularly the Abenaki peoples and their desire to obtain peaceful arrangements with the new settlers over the use of the land. (bartletthistory.org)

> Much of the trapping was done by the [Abenaki] people, and traded to the English colonists for durable goods. These contributions by Native American Abenaki peoples went largely unreported. (wikipedia.ca)

A particularly heartwarming story about the relationship between the early European settlers and the Abenaki First Nations people is shared by a long-time friend and former schoolmate:

> My ancestors immigrated to Canada from the Isle of Lewis [Scotland] in the early 1800s and settled in Scotstown [not far from Cookshire]. I recall my grandfather, Murdo MacLennan, telling stories about how his ancestors barely survived the first few harsh winters and only did so because of the kindnesses shown and the sharing of food by the First Nations people of the area. (Jim MacKinnon)

Eastern Townships Presence

The early presence of humans in the Eastern Townships has been revealed by the discoveries of the late James "Jim" Hosking, considered by the archaeological community as the father of prehistoric archaeology in the Townships:

Abenaki birchbark wigwam
(warpaths2peacepipes.com)

> In the five decades he has lived in Quebec, 79-year-old Hosking has found 27 out of the 100 or so major archeological sites in the Townships from the Megantic Mountains in the east to Lake Memphremagog in the west, and from Ayer's Cliff in the south, north to Bromptonville. He has personally amassed a collection of more than 2,000 artifacts, including stone axes, knives, spearpoints, scraping tools, amulets and pottery that date back centuries and, in some cases, even millennia. (Dwane Wilkin, "Jim Hosking: Seeking the Red Man in the Townships," Log Cabin Chronicles 2001.11.01)

More recent archaeological digs at various sites have confirmed the presence of Paleoindian peoples and Abenaki First Nations peoples in the Eastern Townships. Some of these discoveries are described briefly below.

> Three fragments of spearheads discovered in the Lac Mégantic region two hours south of Quebec City are believed to be more than 10,000 years old and are being hailed as a major find. The artifacts, which will be exhibited publicly for the first time today, are said to be the first evidence of human habitation in Quebec after the glaciers receded and the ice age ended some 12,000 years ago. The fragments are from fluted spearheads typical of weapons used in the early Paleoindian period 10,000 to 12,000 years ago. (The [Sherbrooke] Record, Aug. 15, 2003)

The discovery of a late Paleoindian archeological site near Weedon confirms the presence of North American natives in the Saint-Francis River Valley 10,000 years ago. At that time these hunters may have already occasionally visited the Eaton River searching for big game, especially caribou. However, it was only 6000 years ago that groups of native hunters, fishermen and gatherers regularly occupied this area. This is clearly shown by the discovery of artefacts related to the people of the Laurentian Archaic Culture along the banks of the Saint-Francis and Eaton rivers . . . Natives frequented the region over the course of several thousand years, building temporary camps along the Saint-Francis and its tributaries such as the Eaton River. They harvested local game including moose, deer, beaver, black bear and the few remaining caribou, and fish such as eels, sturgeon and Atlantic salmon, which were all common in the Saint-Francis basin until modern times. (Eaton Corner Museum display)

Archaeologist Éric Graillon, of the Musée de la nature et des sciences de Sherbrooke, has worked for 20 years on the development of research and the diffusion of prehistoric archaeological knowledge in the Eastern Townships. During this time he had led archaeological dig projects in East Hereford, Notre-Dame-des-Bois, East Angus, Coaticook and Lennoxville. Since 2010, he has led digs on the Gaudreau site in Weedon. (Eric Graillon, "Du Paléoindien récent au Régime français : 10 000 ans de présence amérindienne à Weedon dans les Cantons-de-l'Est," erudit.org; translated from French by author)

Even closer to home, at nearby Island Brook, a most interesting discovery was made by a young man working on his father's farm:

About 70 years ago, while working with my dad picking stones, I noticed a stone that was very different from the others, so I picked it up and put it in my pocket. It was about six inches [15 cm] long, had a couple of line markings and

Amerindian skinning knife (6800-4500 BC) found at Island Brook by Robert Burns (photo courtesy of Sharon Moore, Eaton Corner Museum)

was grey in colour. Professor Ian Tait of Champlain College identified it as a tool to skin fish and estimated its date to be about 3000 BC. Further analysis by the Curator of the Museum of Nature and Science in Sherbrooke suggested that it could date back to 6800 BC. In 2013 the artifact was loaned to the Eaton Corner Museum where it is now part of their display. (Robert Burns)

Cookshire Presence

The town of Cookshire-Eaton's website declares that the Abenakis were the first people to set camp along the Eaton River. Although that may be true, no definitive proof has yet been found of prehistoric Abenaki presence in Cookshire. In 2011 the Compton County Historical and Museum Society commissioned a study by Archéotec inc. of the archaeological potential of the area. The study's report listed a large number of sites of archaeological interest, including Pine Hill Farm.

Exploratory archaeological digs were undertaken in October 2019 at Pine Hill Farm on the west bank of the Eaton River to search for hard evidence. These digs were under the direction of Dr. Geneviève Treyvaud, associate professor at Université Laval and archaeologist of the Grand Conseil de la Nation Waban-Aki.

Eaton River looking upstream, Pine Hill Farm, Oct. 2019 (photo by Jim Fraser)

On October 15, Dr. Treyvaud's team (archaeologist Roxane Lévesque and research assistants Jean-Nicolas Plourde and Daniel Ducharme) arrived at the farm to undertake the digs. First they studied the riverfront property's geography to determine the most likely locations of an Abenaki encampment. Then, armed with their digging tools (shovel, pick, trowel and soil removal tray), they proceeded to meticulously dig several exploratory test pits. Each pit was approximately 18 inches (45 cm) square and was dug to a depth of 2-3 ft. (60-90 cm). The dirt was carefully removed in very thin layers using mainly trowel and tray. Throughout the process, Lévesque recorded the GPS coordinates of the pit, the detailed

Archaeologist Roxane Lévesque excavating a test pit on the west bank of the Eaton River, Pine Hill Farm, Oct. 2019 (photos by Jim Fraser)

characteristics of the different soil levels encountered, and a description of any objects unearthed. Items of interest were deposited in labelled paper bags or small containers (depending on size) for later analysis. Once all the data was recorded, the pit was filled in, restoring the site to its original condition.

Research assistant Daniel Ducharme excavating a test pit, Oct. 2019 (photo by Jim Fraser)

Archaeologist Roxane Lévesque examining a possible artifact, Oct. 2019 (photo by author)

These exploratory digs yielded a number of different objects, including a nail, a spoon, a bone and pieces of coloured glass. Of most interest, however, were two small rocks that appeared to have been shaped and worked by humans. One of them might possibly have been used as a hand-held scraping or cutting tool. The possible use of the other rock was not immediately obvious. Both were kept for further analysis and study by experts to determine their uses and approximate dates. Although the dig did not provide definitive proof of the presence of First Nations peoples in Cookshire, the "items of interest" uncovered near the Eaton River may eventually become part of the sought-after proof.

Waban-Aki Nation logos (gcnwa.com)

It is known that during and after the colonization period, some Abenakis settled and remained in the Cookshire area. Local playwright/author/historian Sharron Rothney of Eaton Corner, in an article in the May 15, 2012 issue of The (Sherbrooke) Record mentions "the Abenaki burial grounds just before the bridge on French Road." Recent inquiries about this cemetery reveal that it is located on private property, is overgrown with trees and is closed to visitors.

Land Title

For centuries, the question of indigenous land rights has been a contentious issue between First Nations peoples and white settlers. One of the roots of the problem is the gigantic gulf that exists between the two parties in their respective understandings of land ownership. The indigenous position is very clearly stated on the Bartlett, N.H., history website:

> The concept of owning land was unheard of to the native populace who believed [that] the land was there for everyone's mutual benefit . . . (bartletthistory.org)

Obviously the white setters' understanding was/is very different. Our concept of individual property ownership seems totally incompatible. I believe that it behooves us to honestly reflect on our position.

Probably the most valuable property that many of us own is our house and the land on which it sits. In spite of the deeds and other legal papers we have to

Abenaki window panel display, Eaton Corner Museum (photo by author)

support this "ownership," we need to ask ourselves a fundamental question: Is the property **really** ours? In the words of renowned British writer and theologian C. S. Lewis: "Humans are temporary tenants upon God's property." It's something to think about, for sure.

In any case, the fact remains that the Abenakis were displaced from their traditional lands. Journalist Rachel Garber expresses it very succinctly:

> The Abenaki peoples . . . saw their population devastated by 98%, and their land appropriated by the settlers . . . That doesn't mean they left willingly. It means that the land was taken from them by force or trickery. That's what it means, the phrase "unceded territory." Land that was taken, not given . . . So let us acknowledge with sorrow that we live

on land that is unceded Abenaki territory. (*Journal Le Haut Saint-François*, March 5, 2018)

As mentioned in my Preface to this book, there is a growing awareness of the history and rights of Indigenous peoples. Some of the complexities of indigenous land rights issues are illustrated in the following three passages:

> July 1721 (exact date unknown): The Abenaki deliver a letter to Capt. John Penhallow at Watts Garrison Arrowsic Island by a flotilla of approximately 90 Abenaki canoes. The letter reads as follows: "Great Chief of the English: You see by the peace treaty, of which I send you a copy, that you must live peaceably with me. Is it to live in peace with me to take my land against my wishes? My land that I have received from God alone, my land of which no king nor any foreign power could or can dispose of in spite of me, that which you have nevertheless done for several years, in establishing and fortifying yourself therein against my will, as you have done in my river of Anmirkangan,of Kenibekki, in that of Matsih8an8wassis, and elsewhere, and most recently in my river of Anm8kangan, where I have been surprised to see a fort which they tell me is built by your orders . . . Consider, great Chief, that I have often told you to retire from my land, and I repeat it to you now for the last time. My land is not yours, neither by right of conquest, nor by gift, nor by purchase . . . I await then your reply within three Sundays; if within this time you do not write me that you are retiring from my land, I shall not tell you again to withdraw, and I shall believe that you wish to make yourself master of it in spite of me. As for the rest, this here is not the word of four or five Indians whom by your presents, your lies and your tricks you can easily make fall in with your sentiments; this is the word of all the Abenaki nation spread over this continent and in Canada, and of all the other Christian Indians their allies, who . . . all together summon you to retire from off the land of the Abenakis that you wish to usurp unjustly . . ." (koasek-abenaki.com)

> Extracts from the Royal Proclamation of October 7, 1763: "And whereas it is just and reasonable, and essential to our Interest, and the Security of our Colonies, that the several Nations or Tribes of Indians with whom We are connected, and who live under our Protection, should not be molested or disturbed in the Possession of such Parts of Our Dominions and Territories as, not having been ceded to or purchased by Us, are reserved to them, or any of them, as their Hunting Grounds . . ." (autochtones.gouv.qc.ca)

> Aboriginal title in Canada refers to Aboriginal rights to land based on long-standing land use and occupancy by contemporary Indigenous peoples and their ancestors as the original peoples in Canada. In the Canadian legal system, Aboriginal title is recognized as *sui generis*, meaning it is the unique collective right to use of, and jurisdiction over, ancestral territory and is separate from the rights of non-Aboriginal Canadian citizens under common law. (thecanadianencyclopedia.ca)

Addressing the legitimate land rights claims of our Indigenous predecessors is but one important avenue towards healing the wounds of historic injustices. The recognition of First Nations peoples as the original stewards of the land where we live is another prerequisite milepost on the road to reconciliation. The inclusion of this chapter represents my meagre contribution toward the achievement of these goals.

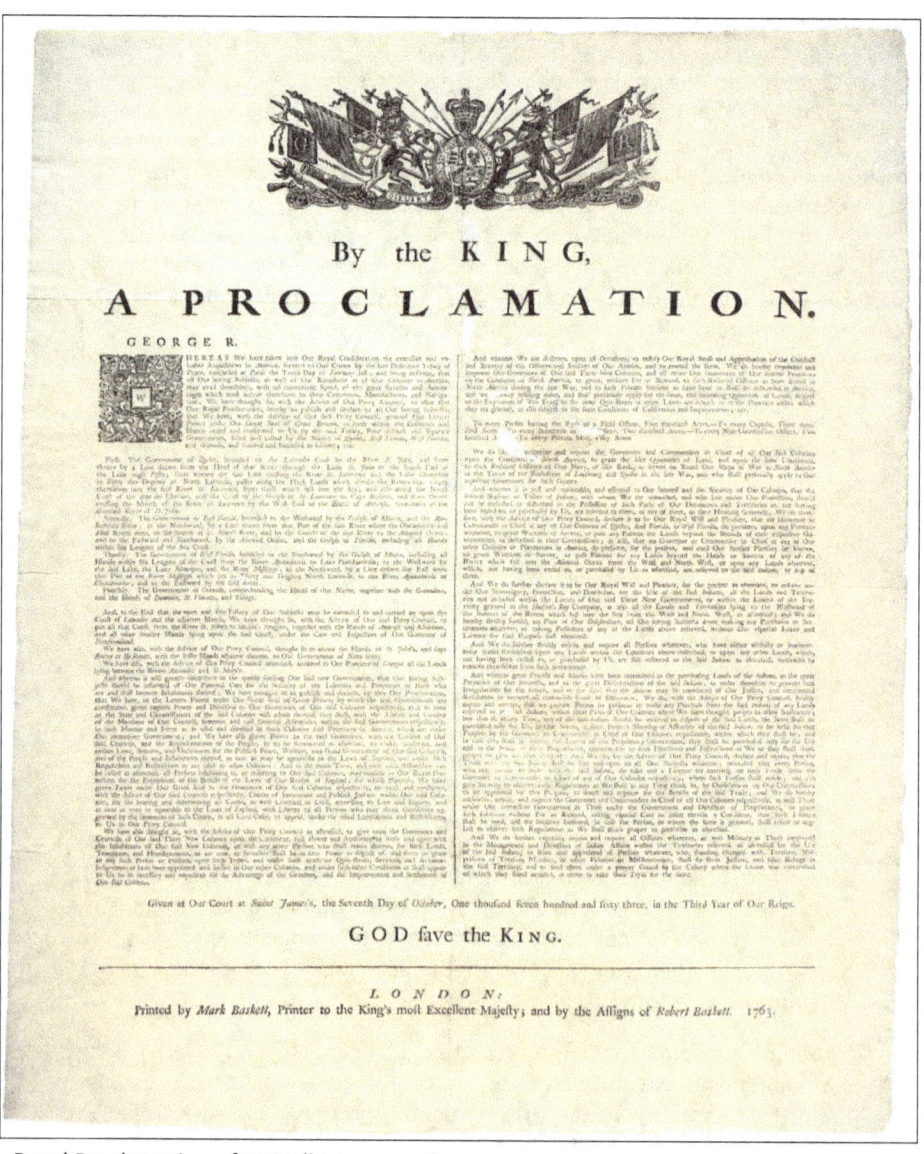

Royal Proclamation of 1763 (history.com)

Chapter 2
Orsamus & Margaret: From America for Land

Silhouettes of an 18th century couple (Courtesy of Antique Associates at West Townsend, Inc.)

My great-great grandfather Orsamus Bailey's arrival in the Township of Eaton in 1797 did not just happen "out of the blue." No, not by any means. Rather, it was the direct result of two momentous political events, one on each side of the Canadian-American border.

Private Orsamus Bailey

The American Revolutionary War, or American War of Independence, took place from 1775 to 1783, at the end of which the Thirteen (American) Colonies achieved independence from Great Britain as the United States of America. Orsamus Bailey was a revolutionary soldier in that war, serving briefly as a private in 1778-1779. He was listed in the roll of Lieut. Enoch Hall's Corps of Rangers, raised by order of the State of Vermont for the defence of the Northern Frontiers. Abner Osgood (who came to Eaton with Orsamus) also served in the same brigade. The exact duration of Orsamus's service is uncertain and became a matter of dispute some 50 years later when he applied for his war pension. However, there is no doubt that he did serve in the war, as witnessed by his badge number 37208432. Orsamus was a child soldier, having enlisted at the age of 12!

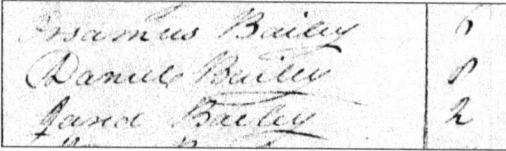
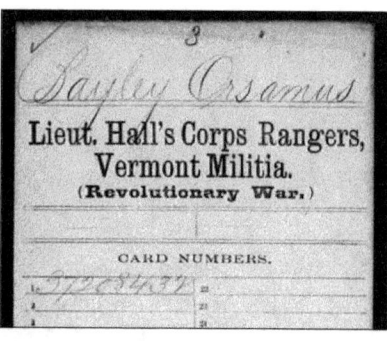

Above: Excerpt from 1825 Census for Eaton listing Orsamus Bailey and his brothers (ancestry.com)

Right: Orsamus's military card (fold3.com)

Orsamus's statement of military service for Revolutionary War pension (fold3.com)

A decade later, in 1791 on this side of the border, the Constitutional Act was passed. This Act of the British Parliament created Upper Canada and Lower Canada and opened the Eastern Townships "waste lands" to settlement. Two excerpts from the Act and the Royal Proclamation of 1792 are noteworthy:

> CONSTITUTIONAL ACT AND INSTRUCTIONS OF 1791: XLIII. All lands which shall be hereafter granted within the said Province of Upper Canada, shall be granted in free and common soccage [i.e., the Crown no longer holds title to the land], in like manner as lands are now holden in free and common soccage, in that part of Great Britain called England; and in every case where lands shall be hereafter granted within the said Province of Lower Canada, and where the grantee thereof shall desire the same to be granted in free and common soccage, the same shall be so granted; but subject, nevertheless, to such alterations with respect to the nature and consequences of such tenure of free and common soccage, as may be established by any law or laws which may be made by His Majesty, His Heirs or Successors, by and with the advice and

consent of the Legislative Council and Assembly of the Province. (swquebec.ca)

> A PROCLAMATION, To such as are desirous to settle on the Lands of the Crown in the Province of Lower Canada: By His Excellency ALURED CLARKE, Esquire, Lieutenant Governor and Commander in Chief of the said Province, and Major General of His Majesty's Forces, etc. BE IT KNOWN to all concerned . . . the Terms of Grant and Settlement . . . (eco.canadiana.ca)

This above-mentioned Proclamation provided the impetus for Orsamus's eventual move to Canada. The story of how he got here is a most fascinating one. But first, a few words on his background:

> Orsamus Bailey was born on September 22, 1765, in Methuen, Massachusetts, USA. He was the eldest of 13 children of Col. Ward Bailey and Mary Sargent. He was married on March 7, 1787, in Vermont to Margaret Whitman of Ashburnham, Massachusetts (born Weydman of Meerfelden, Germany). They had 12 children in 20 years. The 1790 U.S. Census shows him as living in Lemington VT. He died on September 16, 1834, at the age of 68, and was buried in Eaton, Quebec. (ancestry.com)

I had always assumed that my great-great-grandfather, Orsamus Bailey, was a United Empire Loyalist. However, I was to learn differently from author Waymer Laberee's book *The Early Days of Eaton*:

> There is a common belief that the early settlers in the Townships were United Empire Loyalists. This is far from true . . . In February 1792 the Proclamation opened southern Quebec to settlement. This second wave brought four kinds of land-seekers into the Townships: . . . semi-loyalists . . . those seeking fertile land north of the border . . . speculators . . . and friends of the Government. (Waymer Laberee, *The Early Days of Eaton*)

Orsamus, it appears, belonged to the second category – he just wanted some of that fertile free land.

The Josiah Sawyer Connection

Were it not for a man named Josiah Sawyer, our ancestor Orsamus would never have ended up in Canada as one of the pioneers of Eaton Township and first incumbent of Pine Hill Farm. Josiah, also a military man, was the "Leader" of a group of "Associates" wanting to take advantage of the government's offer of free land. Sawyer's remarkable efforts to secure the Township of Eaton for himself and his Associates are well-documented:

> Captain Josiah Sawyer, from whom the village of Sawyerville takes its name, was in all likelihood the first settler in Eaton . . . In the year 1793 [he] set out from Missiskoui [*sic*] Bay, on Lake Champlain, with

A PROCLAMATION,

To such as are desirous to settle on the Lands of the Crown in the Province of Lower Canada:

By His Excellency **ALURED CLARKE**, Esquire, Lieutenant Governor and Commander in Chief of the said Province, and Major General of His Majesty's Forces, &c. &c. &c.

BE IT KNOWN to all concerned, that His Majesty hath by His Royal Commission and Instructions to the Governor, and in his absence to the Lieutenant Governor or Person administering the Government for the time being of the said Province of Lower Canada, given Authority and Command to grant the Lands of the Crown in the same by Patent under the Great Seal thereof; and it being expedient to publish and declare the Royal Intention respecting such Grants and Patents, I do accordingly hereby make known the Terms of Grant and Settlement to be:

FIRST. That the Crown Lands to be granted be parcel of a Township: If an Inland Township, of Ten Miles square, and if a Township on navigable Waters, of Nine Miles in Front and Twelve Miles in Depth, to be run out and marked by His Majesty's Surveyor or Deputy Surveyor General, or under his Sanction and Authority.

SECOND. That only such Part of the Township be granted as shall remain, after a Reservation of one seventh Part thereof, for the Support of a Protestant Clergy, and one other seventh Part thereof, for the future disposition of the Crown.

THIRD. That no Farm Lot shall be granted to any one Person which shall contain more than Two Hundred Acres; yet the Governor, Lieutenant Governor or Person administering the Government, is allowed and permitted to grant to any Person or Persons such further Quantity of Land as they may desire, not exceeding One Thousand Acres over and above what may have been before granted to them.

FOURTH. That every Petitioner for Lands make it appear, that he or she is in a Condition to cultivate and improve the same, and shall besides taking the usual Oaths, subscribe a Declaration (before proper Persons to be for that purpose appointed) of the Tenor of the Words following, viz. " I A. B. do promise and declare that I will maintain and defend to the utmost of my Power the " Authority of the King in His Parliament as the supreme Legislature of this Province."

FIFTH. That Applications for Grants be made by Petition to the Governor, Lieutenant Governor, or Person administering the Government for the time being, and where it is advisable to grant the Prayer thereof a Warrant shall issue to the proper Officer for a survey thereof, returnable within Six Months with a Plot annexed, and be followed with a Patent granting the same, if desired, in Free and Common Soccage, upon the Terms and Conditions in the Royal instructions expressed, and herein after suggested.

SIXTH. That all Grants reserve to the Crown all Coals, commonly called Sea Coals, and Mines of Gold, Silver, Copper, Tin, Iron, and Lead; and each Patent contain a Clause for the Reservation of Timber for the Royal Navy of the Tenor following:

" And provided also, that no Part of the Tract or Parcel of Land hereby granted to the said " ———— and his Heirs, be within any Reservation heretofore made and marked for " Us, Our Heirs and Successors by Our Surveyor General of Woods, or his lawful Deputy; in " which Case, this Our Grant for such Part of the Land hereby given and granted to the said " ———— and his Heirs for ever as aforesaid, and which shall upon a survey there- " of being made, be found within any such Reservation, shall be null and void, any thing herein " contained to the contrary notwithstanding."

SEVENTH. That the Two Sevenths reserved for the Crown's future Disposition, and the Support of a Protestant Clergy, be not severed Tracts each of One Seventh Part of the Township, but such Lots or Farms therein, as in the Surveyor General's Return of the Survey of the Township, shall be described as set apart for these Purposes, between the other Farms of which the said Township shall consist, to the Intent that the Lands so to be reserved, may be nearly of the like Value with an equal Quantity of the Lands to be granted out as afore-mentioned.

EIGHTH. That the respective Patentees are to take the Estates granted to them severally free of Quit Rent and of any other Expences, than such Fees as are or may be allowed to be demanded and received by the different Officers concerned in passing the Patent and recording the same, to be stated in a Table authorized and established by the Government and publickly fixed up in the several Offices of the Clerk of the Council, of the Surveyor General, and of the Secretary of the Province.

NINTH. That every Patent be entered upon Record within Six Months from the Date thereof, in the Secretary's or Register's Offices, and a Docket thereof in the Auditor's Office.

TENTH. Whenever it shall be thought advisable to grant any given Quantity to one Person of One Thousand Acres or under, and the same cannot be found by Reason of the said Reservations and prior Grants within the Township in the Petition expressed, the same, or what shall be requisite to make up to such Person the Quantity advised, shall be located to him, in some other Township upon a new Petition for that Purpose to be preferred.

And of the said several Regulations, all Persons concerned are to take Notice, and govern themselves accordingly.

GIVEN under my Hand and Seal at Arms at the Castle of Saint Lewis, in the City of Quebec, the Seventh Day of February, in the Thirty-second Year of His Majesty's Reign, and in the Year of Our Lord One thousand seven hundred and ninety-two.

By His EXCELLENCY's Command,
HUGH FINLAY, Acting Secretary.

ALURED CLARKE.

Proclamation of 1792 concerning land grants in the Eastern Townships (numerique.banq.qc.ca)

provisions, tools, etc., through the woods, ninety miles from any inhabitants to the westward, and after traveling and exploring the woods thirty-one days arrived . . . in Newport where he . . . began to make improvements, distant twenty-five miles from any inhabitants to the south and seventy miles from the French settlements to the north. (L. S. Channell, *History of Compton County*, 1896)

On 29 March 1792 [Gilbert] Hyatt sent in a petition soliciting Ascot Township for himself and 204 Associates . . . Hyatt at once began developing the land he would subsequently be granted. After selling his property at Missisquoi Bay, he managed with the help of Josiah Sawyer, of Eaton Township, to cut a 40-mile [64-km] road through the woods so that he could bring his family and other settlers to Ascot . . . For ten years, however, Hyatt had to engage in lengthy and costly proceedings to secure his letters patent . . . Hyatt concluded a number of agreements with his Associates determining how the lands would be distributed and what share would be ceded back to him. (biographi.ca, Gilbert Hyatt biography)

Waste Land to Wanted Land

Why was this "waste land" that would become the Eastern Townships ignored for so long before it suddenly became desirable? And where exactly is Sawyer's coveted Eaton Township located? We found answers to both questions – where else? – on the Internet.

Difficult to reach from the St. Lawrence River valley to the north, the territory was largely ignored under the French Regime, which dispatched but a few rare expeditions to survey timber stocks before the fall of New France in 1760. After the revolt of the American colonies to the south, even British authorities chose to leave the land unoccupied, regarding the unbroken wilderness as a buffer between their new Canadian possessions and the newly independent United States. (chemindescantons.qc.ca)

One reason people chose to live in these areas was that much of the land in Quebec was owned by a few landowners called seigneurs. This system of land ownership, based on feudal principles borrowed from France, continued until the middle of the 19th century. The Loyalists

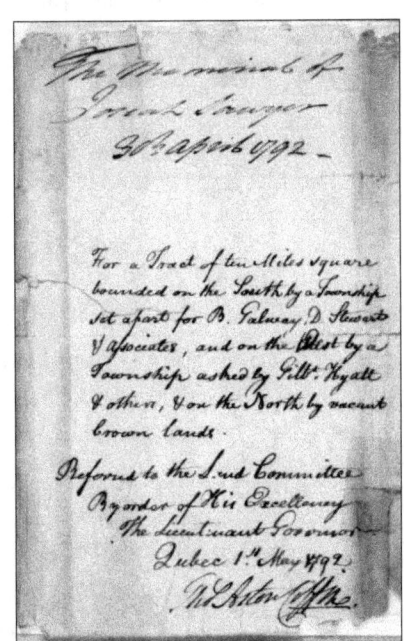

Josiah Sawyer's original land-grant application, 1792 (www.bac-lac.gc.ca)

especially, who had owned their own land in the Thirteen Colonies, did not wish to settle on seigneurial lands and pay a rent yearly to a seigneur whom they had never met. (genealogyensemble.com)

This tract of land [Eaton Township] is bounded north by Westbury, east by Newport, south by Clifton and west by Ascot. It contains 64,685 acres and 3 rods in superficies . . . (L. S. Channell, *History of Compton County*, 1896)

Land Grant Saga

The process to obtain a land grant was a long and arduous one that could take up to 10 years. Anyone without the perseverance and determination of Josiah Sawyer would have long since given up. The first step was to prepare a formal application called a Memorial. (The person preparing the application is referred to as the Memorialist.) Below is an excerpt from Sawyer's Memorial, dated July 23, 1793. As the reader will note, Sawyer goes to great lengths to excuse his service in the war against Great Britain and to profess his new-found allegiance to the King.

> That in the commencement of the troubles in America your Memorialist being then of the age of nineteen years & before the Declaration of Independence was made by the Americans. He was appointed an officer in the American Army, but that upon the Declaration of Independence as soon as he could possibly leave the Service he resigned his Commission & from principle refused to take arms against Great Britain, that this resolution drew on him the displeasure of the Committees & subjected him to be frequently harassed by them. But that he rigidly notwithstanding their oppression, continued to persevere in that resolution to the End of the war . . . That your Memorialist from an attachment to the King's Government, availed himself of the first opportunity of moving into this Province, that he might live under it, for which purpose he came into this Province & settled at Missisquoi Bay in the year 1787 where he has continued to reside since . . . (Library and Archives Canada, Josiah Sawyer Land Papers, 1792-1800)

Among the prerequisites for a land grant was that the Leader had to submit the names of his Associates and have each of them take the Oath and declare their allegiance to the King. Orsamus took the Oath on October 13, 1795.

> OATH OF ALLEGIANCE: "I, Orsamus Bailey, do sincerely promise and swear, that I will be faithful and bear true Allegiance to His Majesty King George; so help me God."
>
> DECLARATION: "I, Orsamus Bailey, do promise and declare that I will maintain and defend to the utmost of my Power the Authority of the King in His Parliament as the supreme Legislature of this Province" (Toronto Public Library)

RETURN of Persons who have taken the Oaths & subscribed the Declaration required by Law; before the Commifsioners at Missiskouie Bay from 26th July to 25th October 1795.

Dates when the Signatures were made	Names	Place from whence they came	Township or place which they intend to settle
Octr. 7th	Josiah Sawyer	Lower Canada	Eaton
do.	Stephen Carpenter	Vermont	do.
do. 12th	Israel Bailey	do.	do.
do 13th	Christopher S. Bailey	do.	do.
do.	Arsamus Bailey	do.	do.
do.	Amos Hawley	do.	do.

List of persons taking the Oath and Declaration, 1795 (Library and Archives Canada)

The Leader also had to pay the costs to survey his desired Township. In Sawyer's case, it amounted to 15 pounds. The survey process was well defined:

> Land was surveyed and partitioned into lots. Teams of men were responsible for this job. Surveyors drew maps; deputy surveyors organized the axe men, chainmen and picket men, giving them their pay, equipment and rations. The process was long. All of the surveying was done with a few simple tools: a sextant, a magnetic compass called a circumfrentor, and a steel chain measuring sixty-six feet. The surveyor used a sextant to find the location of one end of the baseline, and then used the circumfrentor to start the baseline. Then axe men felled trees in the way of that line. A picket man drove in a stake at the start of the baseline, and one chainman held the first link of the chain while his partner walked down the baseline until the chain was stretched tight. A picket man then drove in another stake. The basic unit of Loyalist land was 200 acres, measuring 30 chains wide and 68 chains deep. Every four or six lots this size the team measured one chain length to make a road. Each row of 24 lots was called a concession. A township was usually 24 lots wide and six concessions deep. Another road was usually planned for every two concessions. (Rosemary Neering and Stan Garrod, *Life of the Loyalists*, 1995.)
>
> Clergy Reserves, one-seventh of the public lands of Upper and Lower Canada, [were] reserved by the 1791 Constitutional Act for the maintenance of a "Protestant clergy," a phrase intended to apply to the Church of England alone. (thecanadiamencyclopedia.ca)

Orsamus changes his allegiance (sketch by James Harvey)

Josiah Sawyer land grant: Orsamus Bailey grant recommendation, 1800 (bac-lac.gc.ca)

Another requirement for the Leader was to vouch (in writing) for the character of each of his Associates:

> I declare that I am personally acquainted with the following persons [Orsamus Bailey and the other Associates] all of whom I can recommend as good character; such as I am fully of the opinion will make good Subjects and useful settlers in the Province of Lower Canada. (Library and Archives Canada, Josiah Sawyer Land Papers, 1792-1800)

In a final report to secure the letters patent for his land grant, Sawyer proudly summarizes what he has done to earn it:

> The persevering indefatigable industry and assiduity of Mr. Sawyer the Leader in the Township of Eaton, merits every encouragement. Invited to become a settler under the British Government in this province by Lieutenant Governor Clarke's proclamation of February 1792, he applied for a Tract of the waste land of the Crown for the accommodation of himself and his Associates; and he obtained a Warrant for the Survey of Eaton. To arrive at the place described in that Warrant, he was obliged to open a path through the woods from the head of Missiskonie [sic] bay thirty miles to Lake Memphremagog. Early in the spring following he set out in the opening he had cut in conjunction with Gilbert Hyatt the Leader in Ascott [sic] Township drawn by four stout oxen and two Cars drawn by two horses to carry six barrels of provisions and a quantity of farm utensils, felling axes and other proper tools used in clearing land [of] his settlement at a distance from Missiskonie bay of not less than seventy miles in the direction he took. He began immediately to cut down the trees and clear a patch whereon to erect a hut to shelter himself and his party from the weather; and with unabating labour, suffering great hardships (for the first two years) has he together with his Associates been able in the course of six years to cut out in the middle of a wilderness an extensive flourishing settlement one and forty industrious families, all thriving, who vied with one another who shall show the greatest skill as husbandmen. (Library and Archives Canada, Josiah Sawyer Land Papers, 1792-1800)

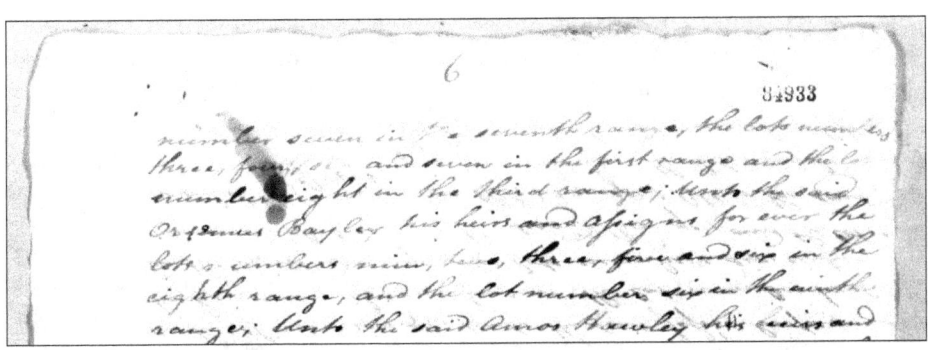

Josiah Sawyer land grant: Orsamus Bailey lots allocation, 1800 (bac-lac.gc.ca)

Finally, in 1800 Sawyer is able to dole out the prizes to Orsamus and the other Associates who had met the requirements.

> Orsamus Bailey – This claimant having complied with the requisitions, formed an actual settlement, and cleared a competent number of Acres is recommended to receive a Grant of 1200 – twelve hundred acres.
> . . .
> Unto the said Orsamus Bailey his heirs and assigns for ever the lots numbers nine, two, three, five and six in the eight range, and the lot number six in the seventh range. (Library and Archives Canada, Josiah Sawyer Land Papers, 1792-1800)

The land grants came with very strict conditions that are presented below by a website dedicated to southwestern Quebec genealogical resources. Apparently these conditions were rarely enforced.

> . . . And provided always and these Our Present Letters are upon this express condition that if the said Grantees, their Heirs and assigns or some or one of them shall not within one year next after the date of theses Our Present Letters settle on the premises hereby to them granted so many families as shall amount to one family for every twelve hundred acres thereof or if they, the said grantees, their heirs or assigns or some or one of them shall not within three years to be computed as aforesaid, plant and effectually cultivate at least two acres for every hundred acres of such of the hereby granted premises as are capable of cultivation and shall not also within seven years to be computed as aforesaid, plant and effectually cultivate at least seven acres for every hundred acres of such of the hereby granted premises as are capable of cultivation, that then and in any of these cases this Our Present Grant and every thing therein contained shall cease and be absolutely void, and the lands and premises hereby granted shall revert and escheat to Us, Our Heirs and Successors and shall thereupon become the absolute and entire property of Us or them, in the same manner as if this Our Present Grant had never been made, any thing therein contained to the contrary in any way notwithstanding. (swquebec.ca)

The written land grant documents seemed quite clear – Orsamus Bailey was granted 1200 acres (486 hectares), made up of lots numbers 9, 2, 3, 5 and 6 in the 8th range, and the lot number 6 in the 7th range. However, the end result was often different due to the inaccuracy of surveys or the striking of special behind-the-scenes deals between the Leader and his Associates, as described in the following two government documents:

> I have already pointed out the importance of accurate surveys of the public lands. Without these there can be no security of property in land, no certainty even as to the position or boundaries of estates marked out in maps or named in title deeds . . . The consequences of this have been confusion and uncertainty in the possessions of almost every man, and

no small amount of litigation. As to Lower Canada, the evidence is still more complete and unsatisfactory. The Commissioner of Crown Lands says, in answer to question: I can instance two townships, Shefford and Orford (and how many more may prove inaccurate as question of boundary arise, it is impossible to say,) which are very inaccurate in their subdivision. On [an] actual recent survey it was found that no one lot agrees with the diagram on record. The lines dividing the lots, instead of running perpendicularly according to the diagram, run diagonally, the effect of which is necessarily to displace the whole of the lots, upwards of 300 in number, from their true position. The lines dividing the ranges are so irregular as to give some lots two and a half times the extent of others, though they are all laid down in diagram as of equal extent; there are lakes also which occupy nearly the whole of some lots that are entirely omitted; . . . I have no reason for believing that the surveys of other townships are more accurate than those of

Orsamus's land grants, outlined by dashed lines, Eaton Township, 1805 (numerique.banq.qc.ca)

Shefford and Orford, other than that in some parts of the country the same causes of error may not have existed. (Lord Durham Report, 1838)

Although technically the Agent [i.e., the Leader] and each Associate received an equal amount of land – usually about 1200 acres each – a private bargain was made previously between the Agent and each Associate in which it was stipulated that the latter should have a certain number of acres – generally two hundred – and should deed back to the Agent all he drew more than this amount. The Agent was to defray the expenses of opening a road through the Township, of building mills, and of having the Township surveyed, the land deeded to him by the Associate being compensation for the expenses thereby incurred. (collectionscanada.gc.ca)

A further complicating factor was that many of the Associates, including Orsamus, set up their homesteads years before officially receiving title to their land. The result was that sometimes their homestead was not located on the lot they were granted. Such was the case for Orsamus, who built his frame house on Lot 10 which was not one of the six lots granted to him! Only 10 years later was the situation rectified, when he acquired part of Lot 10 from fellow Associate Abner Osgood and his son Benjamin. In 1935 there must have been some question as to the original deeds of the Pine Hill Farm property because a request for clarification was made to the Ministry of Colonization. The response confirmed that Lot 10C (in fact the entire Lot 10) was initially granted to Abner Osgood.

Arrival in Eaton

Reference to part of Lot 10 acquired by Orsamus from Abner Osgood in 1810 (Fraser family archives)

Three different sources tell the story of Orsamus Bailey's arrival in Eaton. Although they differ in certain details, they all agree that he was one of the first settlers in Eaton Township.

Orsamus & Margaret

Orsamus Bailey and his wife, Margaret Sunbury, came into Eaton in the year 1798. They settled on the place where his grandson, Charlie Frasier, now lives. He built the first framed house in the Township, said to be the oldest house of any kind now standing. The original chimnies [sic] with the fire places, oven and ash hole, are all standing, being nearly 90 years old. The bricks for them were made on the banks of the river just above the mouth of mill brook [Slab City]. Mr. Bailey cleared up a large farm and spent his last years with his daughter Abigail, wife of James Frasier. (C. S. Lebourveau, *A History of Eaton*, 1894.)

Pine Hill Farm house, the first framed house in Eaton Township, ca. 1898. In the buggy are Orsamus's grandson Charles Fraser, Charles's wife Lilla and their baby daughter Maude; standing is Charles's brother Ward Frasier (Fraser family archives)

Orsamus Bailey and his wife Margaret Whitman (she came from Holland to America at the age of 16) came from Leamington, Vt. to Eaton in 1797 with the first settlers that wintered in Eaton . . . traveling thirty miles into the woods with no other guide than a spotted line, and settling in Cookshire on the farm now occupied by Charles Frasier. There were nine children, four sons settling on parts of the Bailey property in what later became the village of Cookshire . . . [daughter] Abigail married James Frasier and lived on the old home place with an unmarried sister, Almira . . . The only market then was in Three Rivers and travel on ice was the only route in winter . . . For many summers, Orsamus's son, Ward Bailey carried perlash and farm produce in his boat to Fort St. Francis, returning with supplies for himself and his neighbours. (L. S. Channell, *History of Compton County*, 1896)

Orsamus Bailey came into Eaton in 1795. Resides on the lot with his family. (Library and Archives Canada, Josiah Sawyer Land Papers, 1792-1800)

The exact location of Orsamus's original wood-framed house is unknown. An archaeological dig was performed on the property in October 2019 by archaeologists Geneviève Treyvaud and Roxane Lévesque and their team to search for remains of the building's foundation. Guided by the historic photograph shown on the previous page, several test pits were dug in various sites above and behind the existing brick house. In addition, soundings were taken (using Pine Hill Farm renter Marc Nault's sounding rod) in an area below the house. Although no signs of a foundation were found, Dr. Treyvaud made an interesting observation. Based on her examination of the mortar used, she believes that the shed behind the current brick house may have been part of the original framed house. Further research will be required to test this theory.

Research assistants Jean-Nicolas Plourde and Daniel Ducharme using sounding rod at Pine Hill Farm (photo by Jim Fraser)

Research assistant Daniel Ducharme excavating a test pit near the Pine Hill Farm house, Oct. 2019 (photo by Jim Fraser)

The archaeological team at Pine Hill Farm, L-R: Jean-François Provencher, Geneviève Treyvaud, Roxane Lévesque, Jean-Nicolas Plourde, Daniel Ducharme; Oct. 2019 (photo by Jim Fraser)

It is also recorded, in the Josiah Sawyer Land Papers, that Orsamus had built at least one of the two Pine Hill Farm barns before 1800. Possibly he also constructed the second barn, but no record has been found to confirm that possibility. However, it is known that the second barn was built no later than 1848.

In his summary of the status of the fledgling settlement, Josiah Sawyer reports that there are 21 Associates and a total of 120 inhabitants and that he has spent 149 pounds building roads. He also provides a glowing picture of its agricultural success:

> Their crops raised in extensive fields, well fenced, are abundant this year: consisting of wheat, oats, barley, millet, kidney beans, buckwheat, Indian corn, potatoes, turnips, tobacco, hemp, flax, pumpkins and squash. This great abundance for feeding cattle in winter and fine musk and water melons arriving at perfection in the open ground without manure. Garden stuff of all kind grows in great perfection and many young and thriving orchards are to be seen. Good houses and barns are rising everywhere. This is one of the most forward and promising settlements in this New Region, which is certainly the Garden of Lower Canada in point of soil and every settler in it appears to be contented and happy. The various productions of this extensive tract lying between the line 45

degrees which separates this Province from Vermont and the River Chaudiere to the Eastward, must find its way to Quebec. (Library and Archives Canada, Josiah Sawyer Land Papers, 1792-1800)

Eaton Township's settlement success and the diversity of its forests were noted in other historical documents:

> Few of our townships could furnish as many examples of the permanent and successful settler as Eaton; a class that necessarily combined energy, industry, and sobriety. (Catherine Matilda Day, *A History of the Eastern Townships*, 1869)

> The timber is more remarkable for diversity of kind than excellence of quality; pine, birch, basswood, spruce and hemlock are plentiful; that which covers the summits of the ridges is generally hard wood, viz. maple, beech, birch and basswood; on the slopes is a mixture of spruce with occasional patches of cedar where the land is very wet. (Topographical Dictionary, 1832)

Pioneer Life

The following series of vignettes illustrate various aspects of early pioneer life in Eaton Township – clearing and building, travel and tragedy, snow in summer, peddlers and provisions, and love and marriage.

> As was frequently done in those days, the future colonists took possession of their homestead before actually receiving legal title to the land. Records give evidence of Josiah Sawyer and some of his associates living in the future Eaton County [Township] as early as 1793. Pioneers arriving in Eaton County [Township] must have had to pass by way of Missisquoi Bay (Lake Champlain) and travel through virgin forest. Nothing could make them turn back: the cold, an abundance of snow, thawing swamps, or ice break-up. When the pioneers arrived at their new property, they naturally had to clear the land, prepare a garden and build log cabins which would eventually shelter their families. After completing these arduous tasks, often with a single ax, this handful of men went back through mountains, rivers and swamps. The next year, these untameable pioneers defied nature a second time and came back to settle in their township, this time with their wives and children. Apparently their love for His Majesty, the King of England and the lure of vast free land made these Eaton Township founding fathers forget the hardship of the voyage and the work of clearing of the land. ("The Rise of a Country Hamlet to a County Seat, 1793-1900," *Cookshire 1892-1992*, 1992)

> Up to the time of the building of the Grand Trunk Railway, all marketing was done either by boat or team to Three Rivers or Montreal. The Eaton and St. Francis rivers gave the settlers good transportation for those days . . . The boats were sent down the St. Francis River to its junction

with the St. Lawrence, and there, produce was transferred to larger boats for Montreal, Quebec, Three Rivers and other places. The principal article exported in those days was pearl-ash, made from hardwood ashes. This sold for about $12 per one hundred pounds. Flour and other necessaries were bought back in exchange. These journeys by boat were always dangerous, and necessitated hard labour at places like Brompton Falls, where everything had to be carried around on land in both directions. (L. S. Channell, *History of Compton County*, 1896)

Our earliest settlers used the St. Francis [River] as the only road to the administrative and business center of the Townships at Three Rivers . . . The only cash crops of those early days were potash and potatoes – the potash refined into pearlash and the potatoes distilled into whisky – and all had to be marketed at Three Rivers. In the Eaton Valley, one of the most flourishing of the early settlements, there was a whisky distillery near what is now the village of Eaton Corner and John Lebourveau built a pearl ashery just north of today's Cookshire. The produce of each, in kegs and barrels supplied by local coopers, was carried to Eaton Landing on the St. Francis half-a-mile below today's East Angus. There it was loaded into flatboats powered by poles and sweeps for a three-week round trip to the St. Lawrence. (Bernard Epps, "Tales of the St. Francis River" in *The Record*, Feb. 29, 1984)

Original cast iron kettles for making pearl ash at Pine Hill Farm (photo by author)

On May 25, 1815, Orsamus Bailey and others from Eaton took a flat boat down the Eaton River destined for Three Rivers, had to unload their cargo at Brompton Falls. Two of the men, John French and John Hurd, attempted to "shoot the falls" [in the empty boat] but tragically drowned in the process. (*Sherbrooke Daily Record*, Mar. 16, 1957)

These early settlers met with and overcame many hardships . . . The late Alden Learned, of Learned Plain, has left an account of those early days, and he says: "The 6th of June, 1816, it commenced to snow, with the wind from the north-west, and it snowed for three days, the weather as cold as winter. The leaves were all killed and nearly all the birds died. On account of the cold summer and hard frosts for two or three years in succession, provisions of all kinds were very high, flour selling from $15 to $18 per barrel. Many of the farms were left vacant and half of the settlers left the country . . ." (L. S. Channell, *History of Compton County*, 1896)

The pioneers cut down trees, and burned the trunks, branches and stumps to produce potash, which sold at good profit. . . The potash was extracted from hardwood ashes, and rather easily produced. You leached one volume of ashes with two volumes of water, and boiled the water until you had a black cake of salts. These black salts could be sold as such, or baked into pearlash (so called because of its white color) by heating the black salts to 1000 degrees Fahrenheit and boiling them to remove all impurities. Pearl ash was only made by asheries who had more expensive kettles that could withstand the necessary heat. (Georges Létourneau and Jay Sames, "Ash to Cash – The Untold Story: Nature's Burnt Offering to 19th Century Settlers" in erudit.org)

John Lebourveau came from Vermont into the Township of Eaton in 1799, and worked for Josiah Sawyer, a pioneer who became a noted man of his day. John was capable and ambitious; he worked with his eyes turned to the future. Not far distant in Newport Township lived Sally Stratton and soon they fell in love. After two years of courtship, John and Sally decided to marry but there was no minister to perform the ceremony. They made their plans and travelled on horseback, one horse, to New Hampshire (name of the town not known) some forty miles through virgin forest following the spotted trail through forests, across brooks, along winding paths; all these being used by pioneer settlers who went to and fro between one country to another. There were no customs then, when tolls were enacted from people of times not able to pay, but there were wild animals to meet and pass, and much hardship. At the marriage of John and Sally there were no flowers, no bridal veil, no stylish attire for either, but there was love, and confidence in the future, and a faith in each other that carried them through the years. The return journey was made the same way as the first. They began their married life in a small settlement near Cookshire, which at the time rejoiced the name of "Slab City" owing to a sawmill that did a thriving business. (genealogy.com; Lebourveau family file)

Orsamus the Farmer

Little is known about Orsamus Bailey's farming activities apart from a few clues provided in his personal page in the Attleborough Ledger – the account book of a travelling salesman from Attleborough, Mass., who regularly visited the Eaton pioneers in the early 1800s to sell both his wares and his services. Following is an interpretation of Orsamus's transactions; presumably the prices were in American dollars.

- January 27, 1807: 3 chairs $4; one pair of pliers $0.50
- May 3, 1808: walking plow $2.23; sleigh hinge tool $0.58; making sleigh hinge for traveler $0.50; brew trough $1.00; 3 chair frames $1.50;
- March 19, 1809: large wheel $2.00; 3 tables $6.00; Moses Ball 9 days work on bot& billet ____ $8.50; 44½ lb. beef $3.50; 2 bushels Roe $8.25; full table $5.00;

sleigh $7.00; six chairs $5.95; bureau $9.00; stand $2.00; fold leaf table $7.00
- July 1827: three hay rakes $1.50
- March 5, 1828: bed stead $2.34
- June 27, 1831: 12 dining chairs $12.00; One large ham $3.00
- July 10: 2 hay rakes $1.00

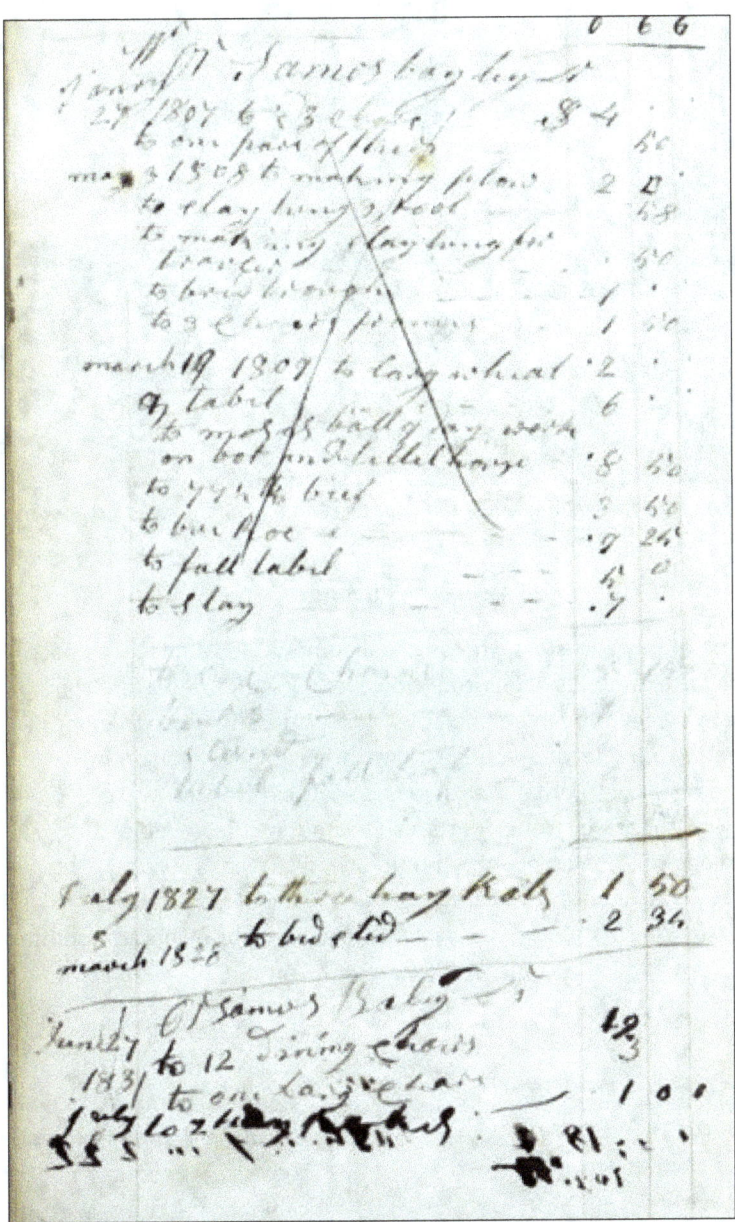

Orsamus's Attleborough Ledger account record, 1807-1831
(numerique.banq.qc.ca)

One wonders whether the set of 12 dining chairs that Orsamus bought in 1831 is the same set that remains in the Pine Hill Farm house today.

The 19th century travelling salesman (Daniel Hagerman, fineartamerica.com)

Passing the Pitchfork

In the time of our ancestors, the usual custom was for a farmer to pass the home farm on to his eldest son. However, Orsamus departed from this tradition. Even though he had at least four sons, he chose to pass the property to his second-youngest daughter, Abigail, and son-in-law, James Frasier. Perhaps this was because his sons were already well settled on other parts of Orsamus's considerable land holdings of 1200 acres (486 ha). In any case, that's how the Frasers first came to own and operate Pine Hill Farm.

An interesting side note is that Abigail's niece, Persis, married the later-to-become-famous Honourable John Henry Pope, who served in Sir John A. Macdonald's cabinet and was instrumental in bringing the railway to Cookshire.

Orsamus's burial record, 1834 (ancestry.com)

Chapter 3
James & Abigail: From Quebec City for Love

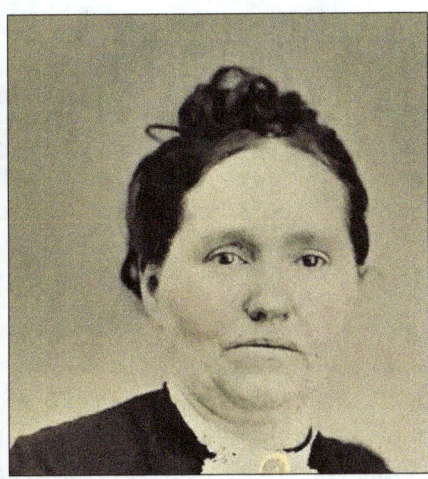

James Frasier and Abigail Bailey portraits (courtesy of Sally Aldinger)

When Orsamus Bailey sold Pine Hill Farm in 1832 to his son-in-law, James Frasier, for one hundred pounds, it marked the beginning of almost 200 years that the Frasier/Fraser family has tilled that land.

Frasier or Fraser?

The reader may have noted the variation in the spelling of our family name (Frasier versus Fraser). This dichotomy has its origins when James married Abigail Bailey. Abigail, an American, apparently thought that Fraser was too "Scotchy" and wished to Americanize it. She had the parson insert an "i" in Fraser when she and James were married. Consequently, all of their children (including my grandfather Charles Ira) were baptized "Frasier." However, many of their descendants subsequently reverted to the original spelling, Fraser.

Scottish Heritage

On August 16, 1790, the twin-masted two-decked sailing ship "British Queen" departed from Arisaig, Scotland, a port on the west coast of the Scottish Highlands, bringing James's parents, Donald Fraser and Jane Dallas, and a boatload of poor tenant farmers to Quebec City. (The ship was probably similar in appearance to the famous Mayflower.) The journey took a little more than two

The Mayflower (theairplanecollection.com)

months. One can only imagine the challenges of crossing the North Atlantic in hurricane season! Unlike most of the emigrants who came on that voyage, Donald stayed in Quebec City instead of moving west to Montreal or Upper Canada. As a blacksmith, Donald had a marketable trade. In addition, coming from a family that appears to have been quite well-to-do, he was a man of some means. It is assumed that he set up his blacksmith shop in Haute-Ville (Upper Town) almost immediately after arriving.

James was Donald and Jane's third child. Although no record of his birth has been located to date, various other documents indicate that he was born in Quebec City in April 1796. Nothing is known of his formative years there, but it seems likely that he left for the Eastern Townships at an early age. It is interesting to note that in his parents' wills, mention is made of his siblings, John and Ann, in the main text, but James (Jacques) is mentioned only in a margin entry on page 2. The margin entry is translated as follows: "Give and bequeath the said testator to Jacques [James] Fraser, also one of his sons, born from the same and lawful marriage, five shillings, for all his legal rights in the said succession without the possibility of claiming or requiring more in the said succession."

Although much is known about James's parents and James's own family of 12 children, comparatively little is known of the man himself. Genealogist Paul Lessard of the Clan Fraser Society of Canada, when doing research on the Cookshire branch of the clan, referred to him as "the elusive James" because of the almost total lack of information available about him. It is surprising also that almost no mention is made about James – or any other Frasier/Frasers, for that matter – in L. S. Channell's *History of Compton County*, even though the 300-page volume contains profiles of some 400 families of his era. The reason for this glaring omission is unknown, but my dad once told me it was because of some bad blood between the Channells and the Frasiers. Whatever the reason, the end result is that later generations were deprived of knowing more about some of their key ancestors.

It is somewhat of a mystery how, when and why James left his father's farm in Saint-Gilles, Lotbinière County, just south of Quebec City. His dad had taken up farming there in 1806 after working 15 years as a blacksmith in Quebec City. It is quite likely that James's migration westward was related to the building of a new

Sale of Pine Hill Farm from Orsamus Bailey to James Frasier, 1832 (Fraser family archives)

road in that direction and the government's desire to settle the Eastern Townships. These possible contributing factors are elaborated below.

> The first proces-verbal of a road in Eaton was made by a surveyor named Whitcher from Three Rivers. This was in 1812, being a continuation of the Craig Road (as it was then called) from the north line of Dudswell to Canaan, Vt., passing through Cookshire, Eaton Corner, Sawyerville, Clifton and Hereford. (L. S. Channell, *History of Compton County*, 1896)

> The building of the Craig Road and the Gosford Road promoted the settlement of the Eastern Townships at the beginning of the 19th century by Scottish and Irish immigrants from Quebec City. (burysimagedebury.com)

In 1825, James married Abigail (Abbie) Bailey, daughter of Orsamus Bailey and Margaret Whitman, and they settled on her parents' farm in Cookshire.

An Even Dozen

James and Abigail raised a large family of 12 children, who together produced 25 grandchildren.

1) Jacob Fraser (May 29, 1826 – ____)
2) James Augustus Fraser (Apr. 27, 1827 – Feb. 4, 1893) + (Sep. 18, 1869) Fanny Maria Rankin (Jul. 30, 1848 – Mar. 18, 1925) + 7 children (Bailey, Jared, James, Ellen, Henry, Charles, Hattie)
3) Abigail Augusta Fraser (Feb. 22, 1829 – May 2, 1890) + (Oct. 4, 1848) Osgood Norvin Hall + 8 children (Maria, Charles, Mary Jane, Almira, Laura, James Augustus, Ida, Jared)
4) Rufus Alonso Fraser (Jan. 10, 1832 – Mar. 22, 1842)
5) Orsamus Bailey Fraser (Dec. 18, 1834 – Aug. 18, 1873)
6) William Donald Fraser (Nov. 9, 1836 – Mar. 22, 1897) + (Jun. 30, 1864) Sarah Malvina Luella Hurd (1836 – Jun. 25, 1898)
7) Ward Alexander Fraser (Mar. 8, 1839 – Apr. 9, 1927)
8) Susan Amelia Fraser (Jan. 8,1841 – Jan. 19, 1926)
9) Jared Cook Frasier (Apr. 8, 1844 – 1913) + (ca. 1877) Sarah "Sallie" Louiza Alexander (1853 – 1931) + 7 children (Ward, Pearl, Neva, Nellie, Foster, Stanley, Robert)
10) Charles Ira Fraser (May 5, 1848 – Jun. 24, 1911) + (Oct. 10, 1894) Lilla J Joyce (Jan. 23, 1874 – May 27, 1948) + 3 children (Maude, Donald, Kenneth)
11) Rufus Solon Fraser (Mar. 6, 1850 – 1900+)
12) Mary Jane Eliza Fraser (Apr. 22, 1852 – Oct. 5, 1856)

Nine of James and Abigail's children survived into adulthood. Most settled close to home in the Cookshire-Eaton area and are buried in Cookshire Cemetery. However, Jared Cook, Ward Alexander and Rufus Solon made the long trek west to California – Gold Rush country – where they settled in Colusa County. Jared married Sallie Alexander, originally from Missouri, and they raised their seven children there, never to return to Canada. Ward and Rufus did return to Canada.

Some of their grandchildren obviously inherited James's travel/adventure genes. Jared Cook Fraser (Junior), Charles Clark Fraser and Donald Alexander Fraser (my dad) all went prospecting for minerals in remote regions of northwestern Quebec.

The 1861 Census of Lower Canada showed that James and Abigail had a very full house at the time the census taker made his visit. A total of 11 individuals were

James Frasier	Farmer	Canada	C of England	× 56	
Abigail Frasier	" "	" "	" "	× 46	
Bailey Frasier	" "	" "	" "	18	
William Frasier	" "	" "	" "	16	
Ward A Frasier	" "	" "	" "	13	
Jared C Frasier	" "	" "	" "	8	
Susan A Frasier	" "	" "	" "	12	
Charles J Frasier	" "	" "	" "	4	
Rufus A Frasier	" "	" "	" "	2	

James's family, 1851 Census of Canada (ancestry.com)

PERSONAL CENSUS. Enumeration District, No. 2 Township

	NAMES OF INMATES.	PROFESSION, TRADE, OR OCCUPATION.	PLACE OF BIRTH.	Married during the year.	RELIGION.	RESIDENCE, IF OUT OF LIMITS.	Age next Birthday.	SEX. Male.	Female.
	1	2	3	4	5	6	7	8	9
1	James Fraser	Farmer	Quebec	1825	E/w		65	1	
2	Abigail "	wife	Can. Co.	"	"		55		1
3	Jared B "	Son	"		"		17	1	
4	Amelia "	Dr	"		"		20		1
5	Susan "	"	"		"				1
6	Charles "	Son	"		"		13	1	
7	Rufus "	"	"		"		11	1	
8	Elmira "	sister	"		"		53		1
9	Laura Hall	Grand Child	"		"		5		1
10	Daniel Bailey	Uncle	U.S.		"		70	1	
11	Ch.s Hammel	Vagabond	C.E.		R.C.		65	1	

James's family, 1861 Census of Canada (ancestry.com)

	Names.	Sex.	Age.	Born within last twelve months.	Country or Province of Birth.	Religion.	Origin.
	7	8	9	10	11	12	13
Fraser	Jared	M	27	—	Q	Ch of Eng	Scotch
"	Amelia	F	30	—	"	"	"
"	Charles	M	22	—	"	"	"
"	Rufus	M	21	—	"	"	"
"	Ward	M	32	—	"	"	"
Bailey	Almyra	F	62	—	"	"	"
"	Sophia	F	79	—	U.S.	"	"

James's family, 1871 Census of Canada (ancestry.com)

listed, including a sister Elmira (Almira), a granddaughter Laura Hall, and an Uncle Daniel Bailey – not to mention a Mr. Hammid who was identified simply as "Vagabond"! What a lively household it must have been!

Ten years later, the 1971 Census showed that the size of their household had shrunk to nine, including five children and two senior Bailey relatives.

James and Abigail family record (Fraser family archives)

Mixed Menagerie

James practiced mixed farming. According to the 1851 Agricultural Census, his 30 head of livestock comprised 15 cattle, 10 sheep, three pigs and two horses. It is very interesting to learn that James raised sheep. As far as I have been able to determine, he is the only one of my Pine Hill Farm ancestors to have done so.

The farm's total area of 130 acres (53 ha) was distributed as follows: 40 acres were seeded to crops; 40 acres were used as pasture and 50 acres were woods or "wild." Crops grown included wheat and barley. The survey also indicated that the farm produced 300 lb. of butter per year.

In 1848, James purchased fire insurance coverage on the buildings and their contents as follows:

- Dwelling house, kitchen and woodshed (80 pounds)
- Household furniture therein (20 pounds)
- Barn (8 pounds)
- Hay therein (3 pounds)
- Horse barn (14 pounds)

The premium payable was six pounds and five shillings.

It seems that James was very well respected. He was also generous. Although he belonged to the Church of England, his benevolence extended beyond his denomination. The following excerpt illustrates this fact:

James's property insurance policy, 1848 (Fraser family archives)

Another note of historic importance is the remarkable fact that the material progress of the Catholic Church in the Eastern Townships was not wholly due to Catholics, for in the records of various parishes are found large contributions made by our non-Catholic friends. For example, the Cookshire Church shows a contribution offered by a Mr. A.

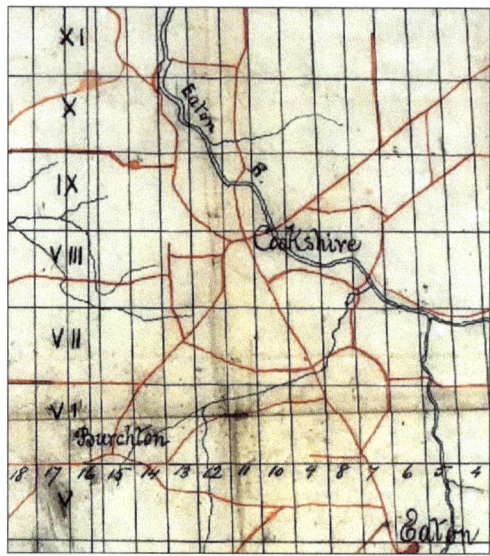

Eaton Township lots, roads and rivers plan, ca. 1850 (banq.qc.ca)

Baily and a Mr. James Frasier; (Rev. T. J. Walsh, S.J.; "Pioneer English Catholics in the Eastern Townships" in cchahistory.ca)

During the period of James and Abigail's tenure, two very important developments occurred that brought significant changes to the farm property per se. The first was the expansion of the roads network. The second, more dramatic development was the building of the International Railway in 1871, which ran directly through the property, effectively cutting the farm in two. The new road of steel separated the upper

International Railway deed document, 1886 (registrefoncier.gouv.qc.ca)

part (west of the tracks) from the meadowlands east of the railway. Obviously the strip of land needed for the right of way was expropriated but no paperwork has been found regarding the terms of acquisition. However, I do remember my dad telling me that, if ever the railway was abandoned, the expropriated land would revert back to the farm. According to an 1885 deed document, the railway property was 98 feet (30 m) wide and extended some 17 miles (27 km) through the Township of Eaton. Chapter 7 contains a more detailed description of the coming of the railways and the impact it had on Pine Hill Farm.

James & Abigail

Dear Abbie

As with James, very little is known about Abigail's childhood or married life. However, we are afforded a few glimpses in an 1868 letter from her daughter Amelia and her niece Martha when Amelia was visiting at the latter's home in Fryeburg, Me. In the letter, Martha expresses concern for Abigail's health:

Envelope addressed to Abigail, 1868 (Fraser family archives)

> Amelia tells me that your health is not as good as usual but it is wrong & wicked for yours to fail, for the cause can be nothing more nor less than hard work – over taxing a naturally good & firm constitution. This ought not so to be, for when all my Canada connections have passed away, I know not where the world can look for such large hearts & generous noble natures as has not been found among them & I hereby plead with you to slack off a little, let some of your hard work go undone rather than kill yourself & thus try to lengthen out your valuable lives both of you & I would say the same to your dear good husband & sons, soon it will be too late to mend. A Norman adage [says] that "God helps those who help themselves." It is thus in regard to health as well as fortune. Now do try & help recruit & nature will certainly lend a hand & do her part. When you write to our Amelia put in a few words to me saying you take my advice. . . (Letter to Abigail Bailey, 1868; Fraser family archives)

Apparently Abigail took serious heed of her niece's advice because she lived for another 20 years! James, on the other hand, passed away within eight years.

It is quite obvious that Abigail's family was a very loving one. Another excerpt from the same letter beautifully illustrates that love:

> . . . changes come so frequently & one after another of our generation is dropping out of sight & leaving us more lonely & more destitute of objects to love & yet as such are removed, our relatives or mine at least turn more precious & my affections cling more closely & firmly to those who are left. We have been talking about Canada friends nearly all the time since Amelia came & it seems as if I should paste some wings on my shoulders & fly right up to Cookshire . . . (Letter to Abigail Bailey, 1868; Fraser family archives)

It also appears that Abigail's family had very strong Christian beliefs. In the letter, both Amelia and Martha express concern for their uncle/cousin Ward (Bailey), who was apparently quite ill at the time. Following is the content of Martha's note to him:

> My very dear Cousin Ward: From what Cousin Amelia tells me I fear that what I write will never meet your eyes but see this reaches Cookshire one more heart which always loved me and sure exhibited only kindness & truest friendship will have ceased to beat but if it should be that your life is still spared let me say to you if you love our heavenly father I have faith in the savior whom he has provided for poor lost sinners and come unto god trust him you cannot fail of a place in heaven. My constant praying is that your home may be in that "happy holy place" & that should I so live as to find at last a home there also you will be one of the ransomed spirits which will welcome me to your abode of bliss and that we may spend an eternity together reunited to all those who have entered those bright portals before us. I thank you my much loved cousin for all your kindness towards me & if I have in any way ever displeased you do forgive. Oh how gladly would I have hastened to your sick bedside had I known your "days were numbered" & had I been so situated that I could leave home but I could not believe your summons had been made out and you must go home. I have promised myself that I would go up to you in the latter part of winter & should could I have told you whom I have ever considered one of my dearest cousins but I must now say farewell Cousin Ward that god will bless & save you. (Letter to Abigail Bailey, 1868; Fraser family archives)

Homecoming

In December 2016 my California cousin Sally Aldinger was given some old photographs from the estate of our mutual cousin Ward Alton Pert Jr. Among them was a very old framed tintype photograph labelled "J.C. Frasier's Father," together with another similarly framed but unlabelled tintype of a seemingly younger woman. Initial speculation was that these were photographs of our great-grandparents, James Frasier and Abigail Bailey, but there was some

Winston presenting the Fraser Heritage plaque to Eaton Corner Museum's president, Sharon Moore, 2017 (photo by Diane Fraser Keet)

doubt due to the fact that James and Abigail had a nephew also named J.C. Frasier. After considerable research it was confirmed that the tintypes were indeed of James and Abigail.

Now that the identities had been confirmed, it was agreed that these historic photos should be permanently preserved. Sally arranged to have the tintypes professionally copied and the reproductions beautifully framed for display at Pine Hill Farm in Cookshire. The original tintype photographs were mounted on a large wooden plaque together with the circa 1898 photograph of James and Abigail's original wood frame house and an explanatory inscription. At the 2017 Fraser Reunion in Cookshire this plaque was presented to Sharon Moore, President of the Compton County Historical & Museum Society, where it remains on permanent display at the Eaton Corner Museum. James and Abigail are home to stay!

Passing the Pitchfork

It is not known exactly when James and Abigail's son, Charles Ira, took over the operation of the farm, but it was likely around the time of James's death in 1876.

James's death notice indicated that he had lived in Cookshire for about 60 years and stated that "he possessed the esteem of all who were acquainted with him." Abigail's passing, many years later, was noted in a local paper as follows:

> One of our well known and much liked "old folks," Mrs. Abigail Fraser, passed away recently. The old lady died in the house built by her father, Mr. Oshamus [sic] Bailey, in which she was born and lived all her long life of eighty-two years. The house was one of the first frame buildings set up in the township. ((Sherbrooke) *Weekly Examiner*, Sep. 21, 1888)

Death.

FRASIER.—On the 22nd of September last at Cookshire, Mr. James Frasier, aged 80 years, 5 months and 8 days.

He was a resident of Cookshire, about 60 years, during which time he possessed the esteem of all who were acquainted with him.

James's death notice, 1876 (*Weekly Examiner*)

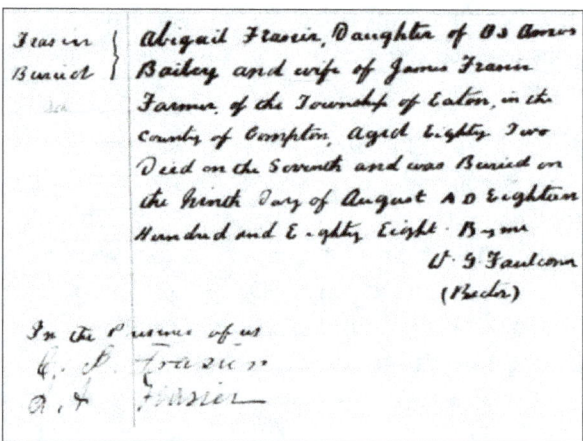

Abigail's burial notice, 1888 (ancestry.com)

James and Abigail's gravestone, Cookshire Cemetery, 2016 (photo by Jim Fraser)

Chapter 4
Charles & Lilla: Bricks and Mortar

Charles Ira Fraser and Lilla Joyce Fraser (courtesy of Charles W. K. Fraser)

My grandfather, Charles Ira Fraser, was the third-youngest of James and Abigail's twelve children. He was probably in his mid-twenties when he took over the family farm. The first census following, in 1881, listed him with his mother Abigail, his brother Ward and his sister Amelia. (He was not married until 13 years later, in 1894.) His short life (he died at the age of 62) was marked by two major building projects: the sugar camp and the brick house, both of which remain as his legacy to the present day. The former will be covered in Chapter 8 and the latter in a later section of this chapter.

Excerpt from 1881 Census showing Charles's household (ancestry.com)

It appears that Charles was a man of means, as indicated by the healthy bank balance he maintained, and by some of the major purchases he made. During the period from 1892 to 1894, his account at the Eastern Townships Bank in Sherbrooke showed a consistent balance of more than $2000 – equivalent to at least $50,000 in today's money! No doubt the cash came in handy a few years later when Charles decided to build his new brick house.

Charles's bank book, 1892 (Fraser family archives)

My grandfather must have been a rather interesting character. As a bachelor (he didn't get married until he was 46 years old), he paid to have his fortune told in 1891 by an American mail-order fortune-teller, Prof. Lebeau. The professor's handwritten report covered a myriad of matters including money, marriage and much more. In spite of the very positive marriage prediction, "You will marry next spring (1892) and all signs point to a happy union. Your wife will be younger than you . . . She will also bring you some money . . . ," Charles didn't get married until almost four years later, when he married Lilla Joyce of Dudswell, a small town north of Cookshire. One can only speculate whether or not Lilla brought a bundle of moolah into the marriage!

Farming Business

During Charles's time, the farm earned its revenue through the sale of a wide variety of livestock, produce and miscellaneous products. The table opposite contains a sampling of those revenue sources together with the prices they fetched.

In addition to the products listed in this table, the farm produced a wide range of vegetables, including turnips, baking beans, carrots, cabbages, cauliflowers, parsnips and sugar beets. Another, more unusual, crop was hops, a popular crop at that time. Although hops have not been grown at Pine Hill Farm for about 100 years, the old hop house (which also served as the ice house) is still there. The process involved in growing hops was not a simple one, as explained in this article:

Hop raising was once (in the 1880s and 1890s) an important Eastern Townships industry but it was not a full-time occupation for most farmers. . . It required a considerable outlay of money for the necessary equipment, not to mention all the labour involved and the uncertainty of the market after the product was harvested. The hop, a perennial climbing vine, was planted in rows and cultivated like any root crop . . . The plants are supported by long slender poles. Hops are used in the manufacture of beer, porter and ale. The hops were harvested in mid-August, picked into large boxes and taken to the hop house for curing. The hop house was a wooden building with an upstairs floor of narrow boards set about an inch apart and covered with cheesecloth to prevent the hops from falling through. On the floor below, a fire was kept burning in a big box stove to dry the hops. When the day's picking was sufficiently dry, it was packed in bales by a hand press. The two-week hop harvest period was a welcome social time for the young folk. (*Sherbrooke Daily Record*, Mar. 16, 1957)

Farming Revenue Sources, 1874-1910

Year	Product	Price
1874	hide	$0.06 /lb.
1875	maple sugar	$0.10 /lb.
1878	geese	$0.05 /lb.
1878	turkeys	$0.07 /lb.
1879	butter	$0.15 /lb.
1879	eggs	$0.10 /doz.
1887	potatoes	$0.60 /bushel
1899	beef	$0.05 /lb.
1899	pork	$0.05 /lb.
1909	cream	$0.20 /qt.
1909	milk	$0.05 /qt.
1910	hay	$3.00 /load
1910	leeks	$0.05 /bunch
1910	maple wax	$0.07 /lb.

(data from Fraser family archives)

New House

Though Charles carried on with farming activities like his forefathers, he will be most remembered for the construction of his big brick house in 1898 to replace the original wood frame structure that had been built by his grandfather Orsamus Bailey almost exactly 100 years earlier. Based on the lack of any documentation to the contrary, it is assumed that Charles himself was both architect and builder of this impressive 5-bedroom, 2-living-room L-shaped home that featured a two-level verandah and a built-in outhouse (in the shed). In fact, there exists a document

Back view of farmhouse, shed and hophouse, ca. 1980 (photo by author)

that specifies in minute detail how the upstairs bannister is to be shaped. The building remains to this day, standing as a solid sentinel on the steep slopes overlooking the Eaton River valley. My cousin Charles, whose dad was born there, describes it best: "Lovely house, beautifully located."

Brick House Construction Bill of Materials, 1898

Item Description	Cost
lumber (2x4, planks, etc.) (3000 board ft.)	$18.83
bricks (60,000)	$104.00
doors (19) and windows (14)	$102.00
tongue and grooved (503 board ft.)	$6.06
laths (800)	$1.20
lime (50 bushels)	$12.50
hair (120 lb.)	$6.00
wallpaper (100 rolls)	$15.00
TOTAL	**$265.59**

(data from Fraser family archives)

Charles and Lilla's new home was built in the summer of 1898. Since my dad was born in July of that year, it means that my grandmother gave birth during the construction period. What a challenging time it must have been for her, given that she also had 2-year-old Maude to care for! During the preceding months, all the necessary materials had to be ordered from the various local and Sherbrooke suppliers. The table above shows the actual costs of the main building materials.

Bill for construction materials for brick house, 1898 (Fraser family archives)

Built-in three-seater outhouse at Pine Hill Farm (photo by author)

Bill for doors and windows for brick house, 1898 (Fraser family archives)

Big Spender

It seems that Charles Ira was a big spender – either that or he just liked the finer things in life. For example, in 1875 he bought a hat for $1.75 – about $40 in today's money. A few years later he spent $5.90 ($160 today) on a pair of boots. He forked out $16 for a cemetery lot in 1889, and $21.50 for a new Massey Harris rake in 1901. But much bigger layouts of cash were still to come. In 1904 he laid out $100 for a new surrey (a light four-wheeled carriage with two seats facing forward). Two years later he really splurged – $315 on a Heintzman upright piano. That hardy melodic instrument still adorns the living room of Pine Hill Farm. No doubt that is where my dad received his introduction to music.

This is not to imply that my grandfather was selfish and spent all his money on himself. Of course, I never knew him because he died almost 35 years before I was born, so it behooves me to refrain from making such a judgment. On the contrary, I have found records that indicate his generosity. For example, his annual subscription for the support of St. Peter's Anglican Church was $5.00, a healthy contribution at that time.

Family folklore has always maintained that Frasers never touched alcohol or tobacco. However, the records I have uncovered reveal that this assertion is only a

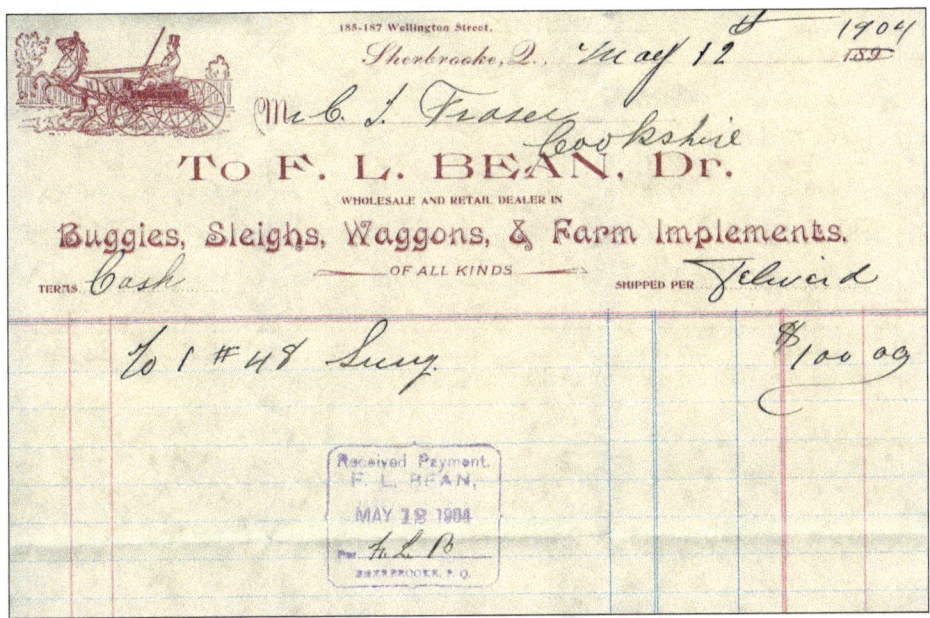

Invoice for purchase of surry, 1904 (Fraser family archives)

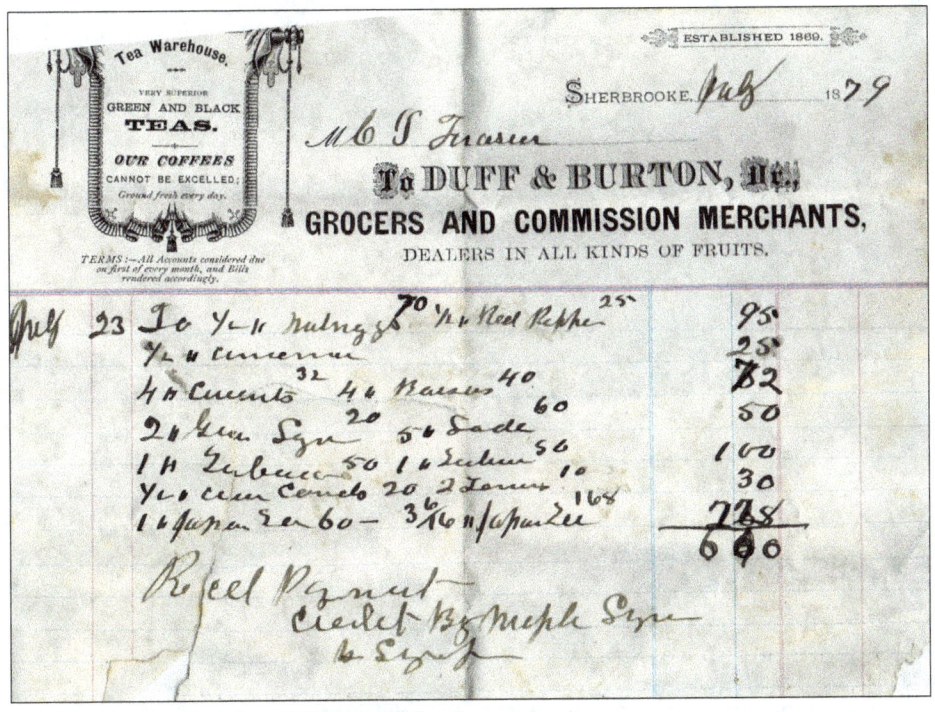

Duff and Burton invoice, 1879 (Fraser family archives)

Pine Hill Farm

Invoice for purchase of Heintzman piano, 1906 (Fraser family archives)

Great-granddaughter Andrea Fraser playing Pine Hill Farm's piano under the gaze of Charles and Lilla, 1985 (photo by author)

half-truth at best. In fact, Charles was a frequent purchaser of chewing tobacco, his preferred brand being Pay Roll. There is evidence that he also smoked Boston cigars. However, I am relieved to say I didn't come across any records of purchases of booze.

Charles Ira Fraser passed away very suddenly in 1911. He literally died with his boots on. His obituary describes the circumstances:

> Mr. Frasier . . . complained Saturday of not feeling as well as usual, and contrary to the wishes of his family went out into the field to work, where he was found dead about an hour later by Mrs. Frasier . . . Mr. Frasier was a quiet unassuming man who by his industry and integrity had won the esteem and respect of everyone who knew him . . . being of one of the oldest families in this section, he was widely known. (*Sherbrooke Daily Record*, Jun. 29, 1911)

At the time of his death, his sons, Donald (my dad) and Kenneth were young children, aged 12 and 4 respectively, and his daughter Maude was 14.

Lilla Takes Over

Upon Charles's passing, there was no question of passing the operation of the farm to the children. In fact, it would be 17 years before that would happen. In the meantime, Charles's widow, Lilla, managed the farm with the assistance of his brother Ward Frasier, his cousin Craig Bailey and several helpers – some full-time hired hands and others who were called as needed. Lilla's meticulous recording of farm revenues and expenses provides a window into the farm's operation during that inter-regnum period.

From the time of Charles's death until his own passing 16 years later, Uncle Ward Frasier was a constant presence on the farm

Charles's gravestone, Cookshire Cemetery, 2016 (photo by Jim Fraser)

Lilla's Farming Assistance Costs, 1911-1921

Year	Help provided	Cost
1911	haying	$35.00
1912	shoeing	$1.00
1916	sowing	$15.00
1917	day's work	$2.00
1919	threshing	$13.00
1920	butchering pigs	$1.00
1920	ploughing	$28.00
1921	cutting ice	$5.00

(data from Fraser family archives)

Typical page from Lilla's Pine Hill Farm account book, 1917 (Fraser family archives)

and a source of great assistance and encouragement. His obituary stated, "Mr. Frasier was always an energetic worker – to him work was never a drudgery but a pleasure."

One of Lilla's most interesting farm helpers was Cousin Craig Bailey, a most eccentric character who lived by himself in a tiny shack on the lower edge of the Pine Hill Farm property on what was then known as Railroad Street. Craig was a taxidermist and a fortune teller. He advertised both businesses with full-page ads

Typical S. J. Osgood debit/credit account statement for Lilla, 1925 (Fraser family archives)

in Lovell's Farm Register. Because he was a bachelor living alone, whose living conditions were not especially clean, children were warned not to accept any food from him or to even enter his hovel. Some who remember him share their recollections of this unique individual:

> Because Craig's abode wasn't the cleanest, we kids were warned NEVER to eat anything coming out of his house. One day, when we were playing on the hill near his shack, we saw the bakery truck stop and deliver doughnuts to Craig, which he then offered to share with us. As we sat on the hill munching this special treat, we soon saw Mom coming, armed with a switch made from a chokecherry branch. In spite of our protests of innocence, we all received a few lashes for our sins. Needless to say, we never accepted doughnuts from Craig ever again! (June Fraser Patterson)

Craig Bailey beside his house (courtesy of Charles W. K. Fraser)

As a young boy, I remember Craig Bailey as an eccentric old man with a white beard. He once told me that he would look in the straw to find me a baby sister (that was probably when my mom was pregnant with my sister Theda). I still have in my possession a great horned owl that Craig stuffed for my dad. (Carl Jackson)

I don't recall Craig Bailey myself but I remember my grandmother saying that he stuffed and mounted animals and birds. He brought over milk a few times for my grandmother to give to the baby (me!). She thanked him for his

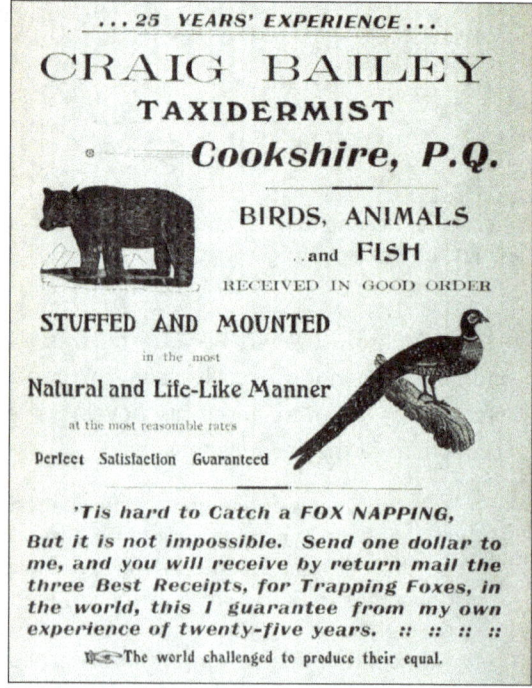

Craig Bailey taxidermist ad in Lovells Farmers Register, 1909

kindness but didn't give me the milk. I guess he was a little peculiar. Apparently some of the boys would play tricks on the old fellow that would make him very angry. (Dorothy Shelton Dionne)

Yes, I remember Craig and his stuffed creatures, including a two-headed calf. (Charles W. K. Fraser)

Another regular hired hand was Frank Brennan who, it appears, lived on the farm for a few years and was treated as part of the family. In a letter to Lilla after he had gone to England to serve in the Great War, he began it with "Dear Ma."

Besides keeping the farm under control and raising three children, Lilla was active in church and community affairs. She was also a seamstress and quilt maker. According to the Courtepointe Quebec website (http://quebecquiltregistry.org/fr/courtepointes/1311), the pictured multi-coloured 80 in. x 67 in. (203 cm x 170 cm) quilt was made by her almost 100 years ago in 1920. This precious family heirloom, that had been in the custody of my eldest sister, the late Marina Tracy, for decades is now under the care of my youngest daughter, Elizabeth.

Quilt made by Lilla, 1920 (photo by Dick Tracy)

Passing the Pitchfork

The pitchfork was finally passed to the next generation of Frasers in 1928 when my dad returned home from several years of off-the-farm adventures and purchased the farm from the estate of his late father. The purchase agreement contained a very special condition that will be explained in the next chapter.

1912 coin discovered on Pine Hill Farm lawn by visitor Glen Gill, ca. 1970 (photo by Jim Fraser)

Chapter 5
Donald & Alice: Indoor Plumbing and Outdoor Ponds

Donald and Alice Fraser on their 35th wedding anniversary, 1968 (photo by author)

Before my dad, Donald Alexander Fraser, bought the farm from his mother and his siblings at the age of 30 in 1928, he had already lived an interesting variety of experiences. In the early 1920s, he and some of his friends, including Wilfred McVetty, heeded the call "Go West, young man." Buying a train ticket from Cookshire to Winnipeg for $15.00, he hopped on the Harvest Excursion, ending up on a farm in the Craik/Penzance area of Saskatchewan. There he worked as a labourer and teamster, binding, stooking and threshing the wheat crop. Among the challenges he faced was the poor quality of the drinking water – he had to add a drop of Frasier, Thornton & Co.'s Panacea to make it drinkable. It is not known how many years he participated in the harvest, but we believe it was more than one.

Around 1926, Dad lived in Montreal, where he was employed as a construction worker by Dominion Bridge Co., building bridges over the Aqueduct. In 1927, he moved to Shawinigan to work for the Shawinigan Water and Power Company. While there, he was afflicted with acute appendicitis for which he spent almost a month in hospital. (An interesting side note is that almost all of his eventual 12 children have likewise had operations for acute appendicitis.) But his most exciting pre-farming adventure was yet to come. Later that year, his cousin Jared (Jed) Fraser invited him to join a prospecting expedition to the Rouyn-Noranda region of northwestern Quebec, to assist him on his mining claims. During his stay there, he lived in his cousin's log cabin. They travelled by dogsled in winter and canoe in summer to manage a network of mineral claims.

Donald (left) with sister Maude and brother Kenneth, ca. 1912 (Fraser family archives)

Special Clauses

In November 1928 Donald bought the farm from his mother and his two siblings for $2450. A condition of the sale was a commitment to care for his mother in her home for the rest of her life. The details were very specific:

> . . . to provide for his said Mother, on the said Farm, a home during her lifetime, [she] will be entitled to live in at least two rooms in the said

Ad for Prairies harvest excursion train (*Sherbrooke Daily Record*, Aug. 6, 1920)

Harvesting grain with a binder on the Prairies (rollymartincountry.blogspot.com)

Above: Jed Fraser's prospecting cabin and dog team, Lake Colnet, Que., ca. 1927 (courtesy of Charles W. K. Fraser)

Left: Excerpt from Donald's northwestern Quebec prospecting diary, 1926 (Fraser family archives)

```
        The present sale is made for the following
considerations, to wit:

        The Party of the Second Part has paid to
his Sister, Mrs. Maud Alicia Frasier-Patton, the
sum of $1200.00 Twelve Hundred Dollars, whereof quit;
to his Brother, Kenneth Ira Frasier, the sum of Twelve
Hundred and Fifty Dollars ($1250.00), whereof quit;

        The Party of the Second Part, in consideration
of the deed above given by his Mother, Lilla Frasier,
hereby binds and obliges himself to provide for his
said Mother, on the said farm, a home during her life-
time, the said LILLA FRASIER will be entitled to live
in at least two rooms in the said house, at her choice.
She has the right to the whole of the house, but should
she wish to withdraw to any part of the house, she
can take for herself two rooms;

        The Party of the Second Part will provide
for his Mother, the said LILLA FRASIER, during her
lifetime, in health and in sickness, a good confort-
able home, clothing, heat and board at his table, or
in her room, should she be sick; will provide for
medical and religious assistance when the same are
needed;

        It is understood that the Party of the
Second Part will look after his Mother as aforesaid
to the discharge and exoneration of his Brother and
Sister, the Parties of the First Part herein, and that
his said Brother and Sister have sold to him their
interests for the sum above mentioned, with this under-
standing that their Mother will be well looked after
during her lifetime, by the said Party of the Second
Part, who will, at her death, provide for her burial,
according to her condition in life;
```

Excerpt from Deed of Sale of Charles Ira Fraser estate to son Donald Alexander Fraser, 1928 (Fraser family archives)

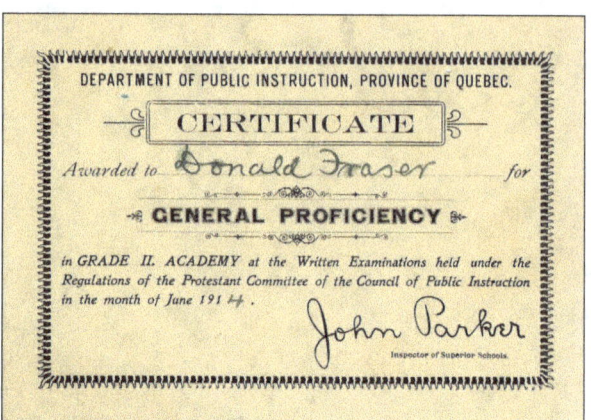

Donald's high school Certificate for General Proficiency, 1914 (Fraser family archives)

House, at her choice. She has the right to the whole of the house, but should she wish to withdraw to any part of the house, she can take for herself two rooms.. . . [Donald] will provide for his Mother, during her lifetime, in health and in sickness, a good comfortable home, clothing, heat and board at his table, or in her room, should she be sick; will provide for medical and religious assistance when the same are needed. . . [and] will, at her death, provide for her burial, according to her condition in life . . .

Less than a year after Donald had acquired the Pine Hill Farm property, the Great Depression began with the crash of the New York Stock Exchange. It would continue for the next 10 years. Although farmers were somewhat less affected by the crisis than other workers, they still felt the economic squeeze. During that period, Donald obtained two loans from the Canadian Farm Loan Board. The amount he was allowed to borrow was limited to $2500 by the previously mentioned Sale Agreement. With the income generated by the sale of various farm products as indicated in the table opposite, my dad was somehow able to make ends meet. Cousin Carl Jackson remembers a very insensitive joke that local postmaster and prankster, John "Barney" McKenna, once played on my parents. He sent them a letter in the mail addressed to "The Frasers, Easy Street, Cookshire, Que."

Some Sources of Pine Hill Farm Revenue, 1952-1966

Year	Product	Price
1952	cream (creamery)	$24.51 /mo.
1952	duck eggs	$1.00 /doz.
1955	hen eggs	$0.60 /doz
1955	logs (spruce)	$50 /1000 bd. ft.
1957	hens	$1.05 ea.
1957	maple syrup	$5.00 /gal.
1957	pigs	$43 ea.
1958	Christmas trees	$0.70 /bunch
1958	corn	$0.75 /doz.
1958	potatoes	$1.25 /bushel
1960	gravel	$0.50 /load
1962	maple wax	$0.50 ea.
1962	strawberries	$0.40 /basket
1964	milk (Carnation)	$49.12 /2 wks.
1965	beans	$0.20 /lb.
1965	pulpwood	$18 /cord
1966	turnips	$2.00 /bushel

(data from Fraser family archives)

My dad was a very shy person but an intelligent, caring man who loved his family deeply. He graduated from Cookshire Academy with the prize for General Proficiency. He learned to play the piano and also played the slide trombone in the Cookshire Town Band. An avid reader, he especially enjoyed Pierre Berton's Canadian history books. He closely followed world events and religiously listened to the daily 1 p.m. news and farm report on CBC. Although he never got directly involved in politics, he held definite opinions on the leaders of the day. It is strongly suspected, through handwriting analysis, that Dad penned this satirical takeoff on Psalm 23 about R. B. Bennett, Prime Minister of Canada in the 1930s:

Bennett's Psalm

Bennett is my Shepherd, I am in want. He maketh me to lie down on park benches, He leadeth me beside still factories. He restoreth my doubt in the Conservative Party. He leadeth me in the path of destruction for his party's sake. Yea, though I walk through the valley of the shadow of debt, I will fear much evil, for thou art against me. The politicians and the profiteers, they frighten me. Thou preparest a reduction in my salary before me, in the presence of mine enemies. Thou anointeth my income with taxes. My expense runneth over my income. Surely unemployment and poverty will follow me all the days of the Conservative administration and I shall live in a rented house forever.

Bennett's Psalm, ca. 1935 (Fraser family archives)

As a farmer, Dad loved his animals and cared for them like children. For example, after a long day of haying, plowing or logging, he would rub down the horses' sweaty backs with fresh straw before putting them to bed in their stalls. If newborn calves or piglets were unable to feed themselves, he would act as their nursemaid. He was also a very clean and tidy farmer with a deep respect for the environment. He kept the property in good repair, regularly painting the barn roofs, whitewashing the stables and fortifying the barn's underpinnings. He regularly scythed the roadsides himself in order to prevent the Roads Department (whose responsibility they were) from spraying them with environmentally dangerous chemicals. (On the other hand, he liberally sprayed DDT inside the milking stable to combat the flies.) He faithfully oiled the horse harnesses, greased the wooden wagon wheel axles, and after each season's use, carefully stored the farming implements under cover. On the personal side, he always kept his barn clothes in the basement ("down cellar") and would unfailingly wash up thoroughly and comb his hair before coming to the table for meals.

Additions to the Mix

Like the generations that preceded him, Donald operated a mixed farm. However, during his time the mixture increased quite significantly. To the traditional domesticated livestock of cattle, horses and pigs was added a wild card: silver foxes. To the farm's friendly feathered fowl of hens and ducks were added less friendly geese and turkeys. To the cornucopia of crops, he added exotic varieties like salsify, citron and popcorn. Later on, in the mid-1960s, Donald expanded into pisciculture, raising rainbow and speckled trout in the newly excavated ponds beside the railway – much to the delight of my mom, an ardent fisherwoman, who enjoyed pulling them out with her chokecherry-branch fishing pole!

Fox farming flourished in the early decades of the 20th century when silver foxes were highly prized for their pelts. It is possible that the fox ranch at Pine Hill Farm

Above: Pine Hill Farm credit-debit balance sheet, 1932 (Fraser family archives)

Left: Pine Hill Farm fox ranch (courtesy of Charles W. K. Fraser)

was established before Donald took over the farm, because his older cousins Jared (Jed) and Charles (Charlie) also had set up ranches several years earlier. It is known to have been in operation in 1933, from an entry in Dad's account book for the purchase of meat for his foxes. My sister June remembers when one of the furry creatures bit a mitten right off her hand. My cousin, Carl Jackson, also remembers the foxes:

> In the early 1940s, I remember the foxes because their pens were near the upper shed where we played in Charlie Fraser's old cars that were stored there. We would sit at the steering wheel of those antique jalopies and pretend we were driving them. But we had to play quietly – first to avoid disturbing the bees that nested in the seat cushions and secondly to avoid disturbing the foxes, which could cause the mothers to eat their kits. (Carl Jackson)

Donald's account book showing purchase of meat for foxes, Feb. 1933 (Fraser family archives)

Although this industry went bust by the early 1940s, Pine Hill Farm's large fox ranch enclosure remained in place until the early 1950s. I remember it was used for a while as a pig pen before being torn down and dug up (the fence was buried several feet in the ground to prevent the foxes from escaping by burrowing underneath). The chicken wire fence also served as a handy catcher's backstop for Sunday afternoon baseball games!

Very little is known about my dad's venture into turkey farming or how long it lasted. One of the things I recall him mentioning was that the birds would sometimes escape by taking flight and would end up perched high in some trees down by the brook that ran through the farm.

A popular social event of the 1930s was the "turkey shoot" (or sometimes the goose or chicken shoot, as the case may be). My dad hosted a number of these shoots. In a diary entry in October 1939, my grandmother refers to "Donald's weekly goose shoot." Such events were advertised in the local newspaper by a small ad.

> TURKEY, GOOSE AND DUCK SHOOT – at D. A. Fraser's farm, Cookshire, on Thursday, Oct. 18th, at 1 o'clock. (*Sherbrooke Daily Record*, Oct. 13, 1934)

Until I did some research on the Internet, I thought that the event entailed actually shooting turkeys. Such was not the case at all, as I was to discover. An online article explains what a turkey shoot really was:

> The Legion . . . sponsored many money-raising projects in the community. One of the most successful projects was an annual "Turkey Shoot" that took place in November, shortly before Thanksgiving. Someone donated the use of some land just east of town . . . and members of the Legion went out and built a trapshooting range. It consisted of a "pill box" where someone (including myself on occasion) would sit inside and place clay pigeons on the trap apparatus. The shooters would line up at their posts and when we heard the word "pull," we would release the clay pigeons and the shooters would fire at the target. There were seven firing positions and whoever hit the most targets would win a turkey. . . . The shooters would pay for a chance to win a turkey and the event brought in a lot of people and money to the community. (Leon Unruh, pawneerock.org)

Another popular event that Donald hosted was a plowing match in 1940, which was covered in the local French newspaper:

> Continuing a laudable tradition, a plowing match was organized by the Cercle Agricole under the direction of the district agronomes and of Mr. Albert Veilleux, Cercle Secretary. A goodly number of farmers showed up at the selected location on the farm of Mr. Donald Fraser. (*La Tribune*, Oct. 30, 1940; translated by author)

Probably Dad's penchant for planting everything from peppers to popcorn stemmed from his desire to exhibit them at the County Fair (read more about this in Chapter 9). When the seed catalogs arrived in the mail soon after Christmas, he would carefully pore through their attractively illustrated pages to make his selections. Garden vegetables and field crops at Pine Hill Farm almost always resulted in good yields – both in quantity and quality. But occasionally there were exceptions, as noted in my mom's diaries.

- September 9, 1950: Dad digging potatoes (mostly bad)
- September 13, 1950: Dad dug potatoes (bad)
- October 12, 1963: Boys finished turnips. Poor crop. (Alice Fraser's diaries)

View of upper pond, railways and Eaton River, ca. 1962 (photo by author)

Trout in upper pond leaping at feeding time, ca. 1970 (photo by author)

Donald and son Malcolm unloading turnips into Pine Hill Farm storage cellar, ca. 1960 (photo by author)

Son James weeding turnip rows, ca. 1962 (photo by author)

My dad was an excellent gardener and took great pride in growing the best turnips in Compton County (and perhaps the best in the whole country). Whether it was because of the soil, the climate or his expertise doesn't really matter – he was the undisputed Turnip King. Perhaps it was even due to his children's wonderful job of weeding and thinning those mile-long rows of tiny turnip plants!

Giant 18-lb. (8.2 kg) turnip, approximately 12 in. (30 cm) in diameter, 1957 (photo by author)

From when we were very young, my siblings and I were assigned farm chores. One of my eldest sister's first assignments was to fetch the cows from the pasture for milking. According to family legend, one day she brought home an addition to the herd – the neighbor's bull. Arriving at the barn, she exclaimed, "Look, Dad; this cow's got only one teat!"

In my dad's era, many farmers butchered their own livestock. Dad was an exception. Perhaps it was because he loved his animals too much to be able to kill them, or maybe he just didn't have the stomach for it. He didn't even cut off his cattle's horns; instead he hired someone for that bloody procedure. I remember only one butchering ever taking place at Pine Hill Farm. One of Dad's farmer friends came to perform the deadly act on an unsuspecting swine specimen. Although I was kept far away from the scene of the execution, I can still hear the piercing squeals of that poor pig. On the other hand, chopping the heads off the fattened roosters was quite another matter. Dad had no qualms about doing that deathly deed, and we kids enjoyed retrieving the birds that took flight after losing their heads. Fowl must have been considered a lower species.

It is interesting to note that my mom's diary often contained code words when recording certain farming activities such as "fixing" (butchering roosters or castrating bull calves) and "voting" (breeding cows). Some examples:

- December 30, 1953: Dad & John fixed 8 chicks
- May 29, 1954: Dad & Percy fixed calves.
- April 30, 1969: Malcolm's heifer voted. (Alice Fraser's diaries)

Horsepower Alone

My dad never owned a tractor, a car or any other motorized vehicle. Like his

"Look, Dad – this cow's got only one teat!" (sketch by James Harvey)

ancestors, he counted on real horsepower for his farm work. To him, work horses were more than a farming necessity. They were his friends — in fact, they were almost like part of the family. Many of them were bred and born right on the farm. All were affectionately known by their given names: Queen, Bess, Skip, Dick and Jack, to mention but a few. In return for a comfortable stall, acres of green pastures and bushels of loving care, these wonderful animals faithfully performed an impressive variety of tasks.

In summer, of course, there was the haying and the many individual tasks

Donald with one of his draft horses, ca. 1955 (photo by author)

associated with it: first, the mowing; then the raking and loading; and finally hauling the hay in the wooden-wheeled wagon. Unloading time meant break time for one lucky member of the two-horse team. The other was pressed into service, pulling the rope that operated the huge unloading fork. Heavy yields, long hauling distances and frequent rainy weather sometimes made haying a very slow operation which could last practically all summer.

Harvest time saw the equines pressed into service for collecting the vegetable crops, including hundreds of bushels of turnips; and mowing a second crop of clover to supplement the diminishing pasture feed. The cool days of late fall found my father and his team of horses guiding opposite ends of the old single-furrow plough. Together, they trod those endless miles, pausing only to turn at the end of each row. At ten miles to the acre (40 kilometers to the hectare), ploughing certainly eliminated any need for jogging to keep in shape! More often than not, the freshly ploughed fields yielded an abundant crop of stones. That required hitching the team up to a wooden drag called a "stoneboat" to collect the rocks and deposit them onto the nearest stonewall or rock pile. A final job before the onset of winter was hauling the bundled Christmas tree harvest to the roadside and bringing the extra evergreen boughs to the farmhouse for exterior insulation.

The first significant snowfall of winter heralded another unique set of tasks for the hardy workhorses. In the woods, they yarded the freshly cut spruce logs. Then, attached to the large double sled, they hauled them out of the woods to the roadside for pickup by the mill. Pulpwood, squared timbers and furnace wood were likewise transported from the snowy forest. Spring was maple sugar season on our farm (see Chapter 8). Horsepower was absolutely necessary for that activity. Soon after sugaring, the land became dry enough for harrowing and planting. Meanwhile, the pastures and fields greened, and before one could say "whiffletree" it was haying time again. And so, the annual cycle would repeat itself – man, horse and nature working together in harmony.

Although my dad stubbornly stuck to the "old ways" of farming, he was not averse to improvements within that context. In fact, he introduced a number of new machines and equipment: the hay loader, the manure spreader and the rubber-tired hay wagon. He also made major upgrades to the farmhouse and the property. In the mid-1950s, with the financial assistance of my three eldest siblings who had already flown the Fraser family nest, he installed indoor plumbing. Goodbye porcelain pisspots, "boom-boom" cans and Eaton's catalogue wipers! Hello soft toilet paper and a warm comfy seat! Several years later he excavated the spring-rich land beside the upper railway to build two large ponds that he stocked with fish. In 1968 he had the house, barns and sheds rewired, which enabled the subsequent introduction of several modern conveniences, including an electric range, electric hot water heater, and oil furnace.

Keep on Turning

Because haying at Pine Hill Farm lasted the whole summer, both family and visitors have many memories of this seemingly never-ending process. In a feature in the August 1992 issue of the Fraser Family Link, my siblings shared their best – and worst – memories. A brief sample:

- I have fond memories of all the silly jokes we told and crazy songs we composed as we turned swath after swath of hay. (Marilyn Fraser Reed)

- I remember hailing the arrival of haying time because it meant relief from weeding the endless rows of turnips, and enjoying the all-you-could-eat ice cream and ginger ale at the end of haying. (James Fraser)

- I loved watching the big old rake and how it dumped the hay in the row each time around. Turning the same field of hay for the 3rd or 4th time was not always a joyous experience. The pail of drink made of one teaspoon of Watkins orange concentrate in a gallon or two of water – Dad called it "Oxydol juice." (June Fraser Patterson)

- How much fun it was to take off our shoes and socks and let our toes dangle in the water as we crossed the river over to the meadow. How often we would shake out the hay, then it would rain, we would shake it out again and it would rain again! (Karen Fraser Jackson)

- I remember falling off the load of hay while crossing the river and getting my **new** sneakers wet. I also remember when the lower barn got struck by lightning while Dad was over on the meadow haying. (Marina Fraser Tracy)

- When coming up the hill with a load of hay, I remember Dad asking "Is the trig OK?"; and hoping we'd finish haying before Cookshire Fair began. (John "Jack" Fraser)

- I remember losing a load of hay in the river; and going over to Green Lantern Restaurant to get the ice cream to celebrate the end of haying beside the pond. (Malcolm Fraser)

Donald haying with horses. Top: mowing, ca. 1960; above: hauling a load up steep Fraser Hill (photos by author)

Top: Donald loading hay with hayloader, ca. 1956 (photo by author)
Above: Children Warren and Karen turning hay, ca. 1958 (photo by author)

- Some of my memories are the peculiar noise that the wooden pulleys made as a bundle of hay was lifted from the hay rack; and being amazed at how Dad could tell whether it was going to rain by knocking a couple of times on the clock shelf in the kitchen (David Fraser)
- I remember the special treat it was to get a drink of Watkins orange drink after the 3rd or 4th load of hay; our dog Skippy eating field mice in a single gulp! (Stevens Fraser)

"Let's keep turning – it's going to burn off!" (sketch by James Harvey)

- I'll never forget having to turn over wet hay, even as the clouds overhead foreboded bad weather! (Diane Fraser Keet)

- What I remember most the incredible heat and dust at the top of the hay mow in the barn; falling through those treacherous ill-fitting boards of the lower barn scaffold, and "riding shotgun" atop the load of hay to watch for trains at the level crossings. (Winston Fraser)

Winston falls through the upper scaffolding floor (sketch by James Harvey)

- Among my haying memories: standing on the back of the hay loader to keep it from tipping onto the wagon when going down the steep hill by Shelton's, and riding on the hay wagon and dangling my feet in the cool waters of the Eaton River. (Warren Fraser)

- One of my Pine Hill Farm memories is haying with three-pronged pitchforks across the Eaton River with Diane, Karen, Warren, Steve and David; and your dad driving the horses and us riding the hay wagon back up the hill where your dad would unload the loosely piled hay into the barn. (Almon Pope)

Author's scale model of Dad's new hay wagon, ca. 1957 (photo by author)

Donald hauling load of hay into upper barn, ca. 1957 (photo by author)

Alice in Fraserland

My dad was the farmer, of course, but my mom was a huge part of the operation. She juggled a multitude of roles, including that of housewife, mother, mother-in-law's caregiver, cook, nurse, barber, bookkeeper, scribe, shopper, caregiver and disciplinarian (except for major misdemeanours that necessitated a meeting with Dad in the woodshed). In an emergency, she even milked cows as well – after all, she grew up on a farm, too. Because her reputation as a bread and pastry cook was legendary, following (on page 95) are her recipes for two of her most famous and delicious pies – raisin and butterscotch.

My mom possessed a healthy degree of "chutzpah," as demonstrated on December 5, 1933, when she wrote a letter to her future mother-in-law announcing that she and my dad were getting married the following day! Although she and Dad were deeply in love throughout their 53 years of marriage, Mom was prone to deceiving "Daddy Dear" from time to time. For example, she always hid from him the jars of Certo that she used when making jam and that we kids were warned never to tell him about. Later on, when Dad refused to comply with the doctor's recommendation that margarine replace butter in his diet, Mom slyly solved the problem by secretly repackaging the margarine in a butter wrapper!

Alice's wedding announcement letter to Donald's mother, 1933 (Fraser family archives)

Baking bread in Pine Hill Farm woodstove oven, ca. 1960 (photo by author)

Like my great-grandparents James and Abigail, Mom and Dad had 12 children, all of whom survived into adulthood:

1) Marina Alice (Dec. 3, 1934)
2) June Elizabeth (Mar. 3, 1937)
3) John William Donald (Nov. 10, 1938)
4) Malcolm Jared (Aug. 25, 1941)
5) Winston Charles Bruce (Jan. 12, 1944)
6) Marilyn Lilla Neve (Jan. 5, 1947)
7) Stevens Hood (May 2, 1948)
8) Warren Thomas Alexander (Jan. 25, 1950)
9) Karen Dawn (May 17, 1951)
10) Diane Amelia (Apr. 5, 1953)
11) David Henry (Aug. 29, 1955)
12) James Allan (June 24, 1957)

Donald and Alice with their "Fraser 12" children, ca. 1960 (photo by Dick Tracy)

Donald & Alice

Donald and Alice 50th Anniversary clock, featuring photos of their 12 children and 24 grandchildren, 1983 (photo by author)

Raisin Pie (as written by Mom for my sister Marilyn)	**Butterscotch Pie** (as told verbatim to my late wife, Becky)
Ingredients: 2 lbs. seedless raisins 1 cup sugar 1 cup water 1 tsp. cinnamon 1/4 tsp. nutmeg 2 tsp. flour 1/4 tsp. ginger Boil ingredients together for 1/2 hour. Put in unbaked crust. Bake at 350 degrees for 1/2 hour.	**Ingredients:** 1 cup maple syrup 2 cups milk 2 eggs Bring the above ingredients to a boil. Add a large black spoonful of cornstarch mixed with milk. Stir in until thick. Take off heat and add a hunk of butter. Pour into pre-cooked crust. Beat meringue for topping with a touch of baking powder.
Alice's recipes for raisin pie and butterscotch pie	*Author's note: Anyone know the size of a "black spoonful" or a "hunk"?*

Even though my mom gave birth to a dozen children over a period of 24 years, she wanted even more. She had hoped for a pair of twins, which she planned to name Cadman and Klinck in honour of two doctors whom she respected very much. We would later question her choice of names, but with so many monikers already used, what other names were still available? Some of us kids mischievously proposed Elmer and Fred, or Howard and Davie, or even Mortimer and Abraham in honour of some of Mom's not-so-secret admirers!

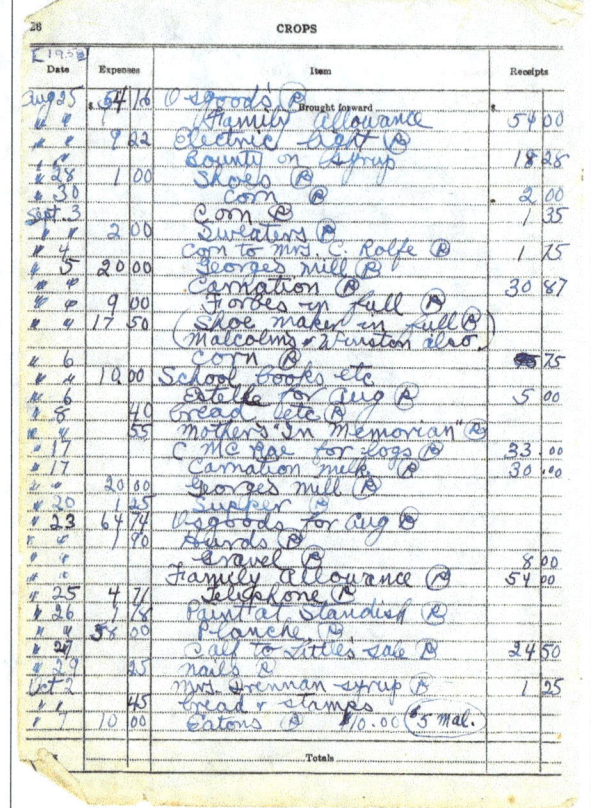

Typical page from Alice's account book, 1958 (Fraser family archives)

Alice with stack of her diaries, ca. 1980 (photo by author)

Donald & Alice

Passing the Pitchfork

When it came time for my dad to pass on the traditional symbol of succession – which by now had only 2½ tines remaining after getting truncated in the threshing machine – there was absolutely no doubt as to whom it would be passed. My brother Malcolm (the second son) had been helping operate the farm for more than 10 years, while at the same time working part-time at the Cookshire post office. Yes, the choice was obvious, but the transition process would prove to be quite challenging – as the reader will discover in the next chapter.

Dad was just shy of 72 and very lame from rheumatoid arthritis when he "passed the pitchfork" to Malcolm. He nevertheless maintained a strong interest in farm operations, and assisted Malcolm as he was able to, especially with haying. But Dad's main preoccupation was his very extensive two-section garden, which he planted, maintained and harvested (with his younger kids' help): long rows of corn, squash, beans, potatoes, carrots, beets, tomatoes, strawberries... One memorable Canada Day in the mid-1970s he and his daughter Karen picked more than 100 quarts (115 litres) of strawberries that one day!

Donald working in his front garden, ca. 1970 (photo by author)

Fraser Road looking toward farmhouse, ca. 1965 (photo by author)

Baking beans stacked to dry in Pine Hill Farm back garden, ca. 1975 (photo by author)

Chapter 6

Malcolm & Doreen: Modern Methods and Community Care

Malcolm Fraser and Doreen Tryon Fraser, 2012 (photo by author)

The year was 1970 and a turbulent year it was – both in terms of the Canadian political situation and in terms of Fraser family relationships. Politically, I am referring to the "October Crisis" (also known as the "FLQ Crisis") marked by the kidnapping of a British diplomat and the murder of a Quebec cabinet minister. On the home front there was the challenge of negotiating an amicable agreement for Malcolm to purchase Pine Hill Farm. Direct discussions between my dad and my brother were doomed from the start, mainly because of the personalities involved. Both men were very shy, extremely stubborn and had great difficulty communicating with each other. This made it virtually impossible for them to have any meaningful negotiations. In the end, some of my siblings and I were able to help bridge the communication gap and work out the terms of an agreement that was signed on May 11, 1970. Malcolm purchased the farm for $23,000 and Dad

Pine Hill Farm

Agreement of Sale of Pine Hill Farm from Donald Fraser to Malcolm Fraser, 1970 (Fraser family archives)

retained the farmhouse together with one acre (0.4 ha) of land. Some years later, Malcolm would acquire additional acreage: on the main farm, approximately 15 acres (6 ha) just east of the sugar bush; and on the meadowlands, approximately 20 acres (8 ha) just upriver. Both acquired plots were adjacent to the existing Pine Hill Farm lands.

For the first 20 years that Malcolm owned Pine Hill Farm, he operated it remotely as Mom and Dad were still living in the farmhouse. Not only was that a challenge logistically; it must also have been an uncomfortable situation for him to be working under constant parental watch, especially given the tenuous relationship with his dad. During that period, he and his first wife, Janice Curtis, and their son

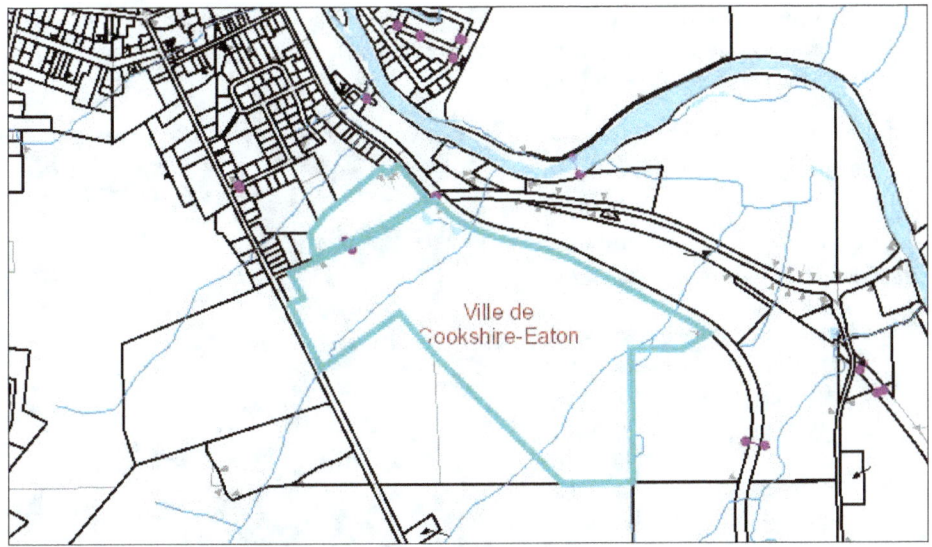
Cadastral outline of Pine Hill Farm main farm (sigale.ca)

Doreen's potato garden, ca. 2004 (photo by Doreen Fraser)

Tim lived in a house on Craig Street at the top of Fraser Road. In 1989, two years after the passing of both our parents, Malcolm and his second wife, Doreen Tryon, moved onto the Pine Hill Farm property and into the farm house. Doreen describes the renovations that preceded the move:

> We moved to the Fraser farmhouse in June 1989 after months of repair/ refurbishing, countless hours of work by [brother-in-law] Dick Tracy and

[cousin] Roland Lowry replacing all the porch floors and much of the shed roof, and [cousin] Theda Lowry wallpapering the dining room and the living rooms. (Doreen Fraser)

After lying dormant for a few years, the fertile garden plot behind the house came back to life, thanks to Doreen's very green thumb. She describes her gardening activities:

> I enjoyed gardening and trying different tomato and potato varieties. Except for some rototilling, all work was done "by hand" – including picking potato bugs – in our garden and in Winston's neighbouring patch. I also enjoyed flowers here and there, around/between the old pine tree roots! (Doreen Fraser)

Sweet peas beside Pine Hill Farm farmhouse window, ca. 2010 (photo by Doreen Fraser)

During Malcolm and Doreen's time, the view of the farmhouse from the road changed dramatically. Doreen explains:

> During our first few years there, all the huge pine trees (there were 10 of them) except one (the "top" one) were lost to the elements – wind, lightning and rot. The one nearest the house was the last one to go. It was taken down by Mills Tree Service as a precaution after discovering that its trunk was hollow. The disappearance of these trees represented quite a change. (Doreen Fraser)

Two of the great white pines were more than 100 years old, as they were shown as mature trees in the circa 1898 photograph of the original wood frame farmhouse. The pine nearest the house grew to massive dimensions: more than 5 ft. (1.5 m) in diameter and 16 ft. (4.7 m) in circumference.

Boy Farmer

Malcolm knew from a very young age that he wanted to be a farmer. He recalls what launched him on the road to achieving that goal:

> In the summer of 1955, when I was just 13 years old, my oldest brother, John, had just completed high school and was offered a job in Montreal. He had a heifer calf that he was planning to show in the Calf Club at the Cookshire Fair in August. Local County Agronome, Donald MacMillan

Cutting down the big white pine tree, 1995 (photo by Doreen Fraser)

The 4-H Pledge

I pledge my head to clearer thinking,
my heart to greater loyalty,
my hands to larger service,
my health to better living,
for my club, my community and my country.

(who would become my mentor and close friend), told me that I could train and show John's calf myself. That gesture put me on a road from which I never turned back. Mr. MacMillan took me under his wing and chauffeured me to Calf Club meetings, Achievement Days and judging competitions. Being a man who strongly believed in the Calf Club (later the 4-H Club) organization, he gave up two of his Saturdays a month to take a very shy teenager to look for a purebred calf. A couple of years later, he took me out to find a purebred bull. By the end of my 4-H Club years, he made sure that I had the training and self-confidence that allowed me to win the Provincial Beef Judging competition and a trip to the Royal Winter Fair in Toronto. Later on, Mr. Macmillan encouraged me to get involved in several farm-related organizations including the local Agricultural Society, the Farm Forum and the Quebec Farmers Association (QFA). To me, this man personified the 4-H Pledge. (Malcolm Fraser)

Mechanization

As alluded to in the previous chapter, Malcolm had already been an active partner in Pine Hill Farm's operation for many years before acquiring the farm. Around 1960, as Dad began to slow down, Malcolm took on more and more responsibility. He enthusiastically embraced farming and was the initiator of many advances in the farming methods used. In fact, it is safe to say that he introduced more changes during his tenure than did all his ancestor predecessors combined. Among the machinery, tools and

Malcolm on his new Cockshutt tractor, ca. 1960 (Fraser family archives)

Agronome D. J. MacMillan and Malcolm with 4-H beef judging trophy, 1960 (Fraser family archives)

techniques he brought to Pine Hill Farm for the first time: the tractor, the pickup truck, the baler, the chainsaw, barn ventilators and purebred livestock – to name but a few. Truly he singlehandedly brought Pine Hill Farm into the age of modern agriculture. In addition to modernizing the farming methods, Malcolm undertook some important building projects. The first was to build a new dome-shaped corrugated steel machine shed to house his newly acquired farm equipment. Then he added a large extension to the upper barn in order to accommodate his growing herd of purebred polled Hereford cattle. Finally, he replaced the rickety bridge over the brook with a large culvert to facilitate all-seasons access to the woodlands, including the sugar bush.

Of all Malcolm's farming equipment purchases, his blue Chevrolet C10 pickup truck was his pride and joy. Over the years, it took him everywhere – to the off-site rented pasture in Brookbury, to Bulwer for

QFA meetings and to Church on Sundays. However, one fine evening, very soon after he had bought it, his pickup decided to take a little trip on its own. It was parked on the side of the road near the barn, when suddenly it took off. As Malcolm watched in helpless horror, his pristine pickup powered its way through the gate and down the pasture before plunging into the perfectly positioned pond! From that time on, his farmer friends continually ribbed him about his Pine Hill Farm truck wash.

Malcolm with his Chevrolet C10 pickup truck, ca. 1980 (photo by author, retouched by Greg Beck)

Malcolm's farming advancements did not happen without difficulties and indeed opposition. After all, if four-legged horsepower was good enough for four previous generations, why change now? In spite of these hurdles, Malcolm forged ahead. With Doreen's able help, he ran a successful farming operation for several decades.

Malcolm's new pickup takes a plunge into the pond! (sketch by James Harvey)

Purebred Herd

Over the years, from modest beginnings, Malcolm built a quality purebred polled Hereford herd, eventually numbering some 40 head. He was a very proud polled Hereford breeder and proclaimed his pride with a large sign on the front of the upper barn, hand-painted by our Uncle Ken Fraser. One of his young heifers was featured on the cover of Polled Hereford World in the magazine's March 1983 issue.

There was one animal in Malcolm's herd that deserves a special mention. The cow's name was Uranium; she was Malcolm's special pet from when she was a little calf until she entered Hereford Heaven many years later. She was the only bovine I knew of that would answer to its name, like a canine does. She could be in the far pasture half a mile away and all that Malcolm had to do was to shout "U-RAN-I-UM" and she would instantly come running to him!

Malcolm with pet Hereford "Uranium." Top: in front yard, ca. 1961 (photo by author); above: in pasture, 1970 (photo by Janice Fraser)

Installing culvert to replace wooden bridge over brook, ca. 1990 (photo by Doreen Fraser)

Left: Installing Pine Hill Farm Polled Hereford Breeder sign, 1989 (photo by author)
Right: Malcolm's heifer featured on magazine cover (Polled Hereford World, Mar. 1983)

Malcolm's Hereford herd in lower pasture, ca. 2004 (photo by Doreen Fraser)

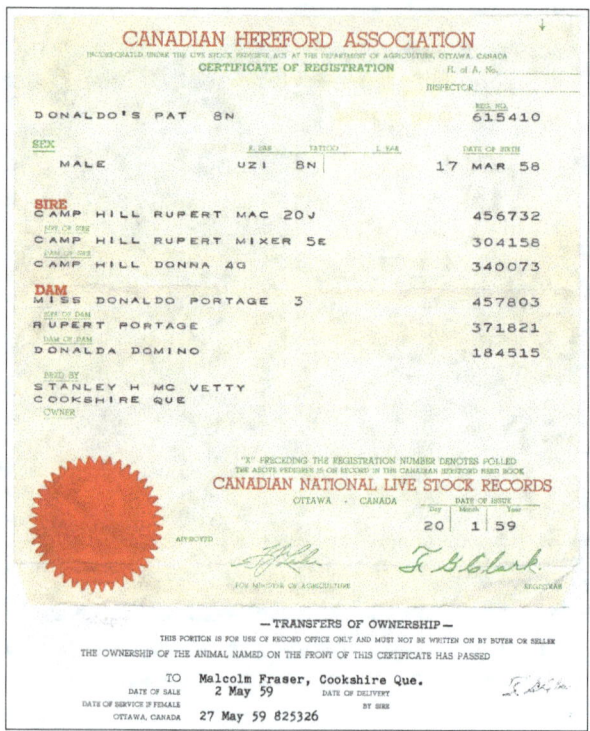

Top: Certificate for Malcolm's first purebred Hereford bull, 1959 (Fraser family archives)
Above: Pine Hill Farm hosts plowing match on meadow, ca. 1990 (photo by author)

Malcolm shovelling manure into manure spreader, Dad on tractor; ca. 1965 (photo by author)

Malcolm and Dad cutting tree with chainsaw, ca. 1958 (photo by author)

Postmaster and Toastmaster

In parallel with running the farm, Malcolm became a very respected leader in the QFA, the Quebec Ploughman's Association and the Compton County Agricultural Society (Cookshire Fair). For the next twenty years, Malcolm's farming activities were in addition to his full-time job as Cookshire postmaster and his volunteer leadership roles at St. Paul's Rest Home, St. Peter's Church and Compton County Historical Society. He also served a term on the Cookshire Town Council from 1970 to 1975.

Strange as it may seem to say, Malcolm farmed full-time but he was not a full-time farmer. As indicated earlier, at the time when he bought the farm, he was working part-time at the post office. That was challenging enough. But, in 1974 he became postmaster – a full-time job. Doreen explains the special challenges involved in juggling two full-time occupations:

> Because Mac was working full-time at the post office, all the farm work had to be done around those work hours. Getting haying done during his summer vacation time was very tricky. All farm work centered around the cattle – stabling/calving, pasturing, plowing/grain and haying. (Doreen Fraser)

One would have thought that, years later, when he retired from his job as postmaster, Malcolm could settle into a slower pace. But such was not to be the case, as Doreen relates:

> Mac retired from the post office in 1992. That gave him more time for the farm and his many "charity" jobs:
> - St. Peter's Anglican Church
> - St. Paul's Rest Home
> - Compton County Agricultural Society / Cookshire Fair / Fall Seed Fair
> - Town of Cookshire activities (e.g. Centennial celebrations and book)
> - Sherbrooke/Compton Plowman's Association
> - Eaton Corner Museum / Compton County Historical & Museum Society
> - Quebec Farmers' Association (Bulwer Branch and Provincial Executive)
> - Bulwer Community Centre
>
> I worked for St. Peter's, St. Paul's (teas/baking), plowing match (baking/card party fundraisers) and the annual BBQ fundraiser at the Cookshire fairgrounds. (Doreen Fraser)

The story of Malcolm's improbable development into a community leader is a very interesting one. As a child, he was painfully shy, rather awkward and quite uncommunicative. He was "different" from the rest of us. For example, he was the only one of 12 siblings who was left-handed (and he remained a lefty in spite of schoolteachers' "correction" attempts), and the only one of us who had to wear glasses as a child. Also, he cheered for the Boston Bruins while the rest of us were loyal Montreal Canadiens fans. So it was with much surprise and even greater pride that we saw our brother develop into such an effective community leader.

Malcolm's outstanding volunteer services did not go unnoticed or unrecognized. Although this humble man sought neither awards nor recognition, he nonetheless was the recipient of both for his life-long dedication to improving the lives of others:

- 2002: Outstanding Townshipper Award by the Townshippers' Association for volunteerism
- 2003: Queen Elizabeth II Golden Jubilee Medal by the Government of Canada for volunteerism
- 2010: Long service recognition by the Quebec Farmers Association (QFA) for 50 years' service, 1960–2010
- 2012: Volunteer of the Year by the Canadian Association of Fairs & Exhibitions (55 years' service to Cookshire Fair, 1957–2012)
- 2013: Life member of the Board of Directors of St. Paul's Rest Home (served as President for 20 years, 1993–2012)
- 2013: Queen Elizabeth II Diamond Jubilee Medal by the Government of Canada for volunteerism
- 2017: Special recognition at St. Peter's Church 150th Anniversary for his many years as warden, treasurer and lay reader.
- 2018: Sovereign's Medal for Volunteers by the Governor-General of Canada

Compton-Stanstead MP David Price presents Mac with Queen's Golden Jubilee medal, 2003 (Fraser family archives)

Malcolm had a particular affinity for the QFA, as indicated in a 2011 interview with *The Record*:

Malcolm's most-recent award, the Sovereign's Medal for Volunteers, 2018

> There's no question about it! Although Malcolm Fraser is neither tall nor husky, anyone trying to fill his shoes or follow his footsteps would find them far too large to fit. The Quebec Farmers' Association honoured Malcolm Fraser with a special presentation last fall at their annual meeting . . . This is his story – a tale of devotion and determination and dedication to family, farming and community and all that steadfast determination to make things better entails. "I guess my dad figured a big family could be a great help on our farm," Fraser says, that twinkle in sharp blue eyes belying his words. But the family farm is perched on some of the steepest terrain on the edge of town here and local legends tell of the stubborn determination of those first settlers to clear the hardwood slopes and as quickly as possible, turn over that sod and get started on some honest-to-goodness farming traditions.
>
> . . .
>
> "And I remember my folks getting ready to listen to the Quebec Farm Radio Forum. Meetings were rotated among the members, sometimes at a dairy producer, another week perhaps a beef producer or a neighbour in the business of raising broilers or eking out a living with two or three thousand laying hens." He recalls everyone listening to CBC, with Galen Driver hosting the weekly meeting, commenting on the questionnaires he had received since the last meeting and explaining the new questionnaire each member family had received prior to the meeting. "Then, when I became a regular member, the Farm Forum had changed to the Quebec Farmers' Association. Meetings were always held in the Bulwer school, guest speakers were often featured, short courses on a wide variety of agricultural subjects were also periodically offered and we were quite a strong group," he describes, adding [that] dwindling farming population, busy family schedules and just about any question [now] answered on the Internet have decimated membership rolls in recent years. (*The Record*, Aug. 18, 2011)

In accepting the QFA honour, Malcolm gave special credit to his parents:

> If I have been an asset to the community at large and especially to my own community, it is in large part due to my now deceased parents. The Fraser family in Cookshire was large – 12 of us – (I am # 4). Whenever someone in town needed a helping hand – to split wood, remove ashes, shovel snow, get mail, take off storm windows or babysit, one of us was volunteered. My folks always said "Help someone else if they need it, the farm work can wait a few minutes." (Malcolm Fraser)

Malcolm and Dad pose beside Cockshutt tractor, ca. 1960 (Fraser family archives)

In his various community leadership activities, Malcolm saw his role at meetings to be two-fold. First and foremost, he acted as an information provider, and he excelled at it. He always thoroughly researched the subject at hand to supplement his own knowledge. However, his secondary role – that of an entertainer – was what most endeared him to his audiences. Cousin Carl Jackson notes, "He was quite a speaker with a penchant for humour." Without fail he would always inject some spice into his talks, whether it be a joke, a poem, some words of wisdom or a good-natured poke at one of his fellow farmers. Here are two examples:

> I am only one, but still I am one
> I cannot do everything, but still
> I can do something and because
> I cannot do everything
> I will not refuse to do
> The something that I can do. (Edward Hale)

A couple of hunters chartered a plane to be dropped off in a remote area to go moose hunting. Two weeks later, when the pilot returned to pick them up, he saw the two moose they had bagged and said, "I told you fellows that I could only take you and **one** moose – you'll have to leave the other one behind." "But we did it last year in a plane this size," protested one of the hunters, "and the pilot let us take both moose."

"Well," said the pilot, "if you did it last year, I guess we can do it again." So the hunters and both moose were loaded in and the plane took off. Because of the heavy load, it had difficulty climbing and ended up crashing into a nearby hillside. After the crash, the men climbed out and began looking around. "Where are we?" one asked the other. His companion looked all around then finally said, "I think we got about half a mile further than last year!" (author unknown)

Fraser Reunions

Soon after the passing of Mom and Dad in 1987, we siblings decided to hold an annual summer family reunion. We felt that there was a real danger of our family drifting apart because our parents had been the glue that kept it together. Year after year, Malcolm and Doreen hosted these popular events at the Pine Hill Farm homestead. In spite of the busyness of farm activities, they were always ready and eager to welcome the 50-75 guests who attended. Malcolm, a licensed lay reader in the Anglican Church, also conducted a Sunday morning memorial church service to begin the reunion celebrations. Following is an excerpt from his address at one such service:

> What an appropriate hymn [Unto the Hills] that we have just sung for this service where many of Donald and Alice Fraser's descendants are present. Let us think for a few moments on the first line, "Unto the hills around do I lift up my longing eyes." All my brothers and sisters are well aware of where the kitchen is situated at the farm house. Two big windows look out towards the hills in the east, past the Eaton River valley with Megantic Mountain visible in the distance. The other kitchen window and the front door face the hills to the north called the Stoke Range. First thing in the morning, our parents could look out on the hills, see the sun rise and give thanks to the Lord for another day... Let us go back another generation to the time of my grandparents, Charles Ira Fraser and Lilla Joyce, as they were making plans to build their new brick house. They must have either pondered the 121st Psalm or recently fallen in love with this hymn, as it was written in 1877. How much thought, hope and prayer must have gone into that undertaking where they not only built a beautiful and sturdy brick house, but put the kitchen – the focal point of any farm house – and their master bedroom with windows facing the hills in the East . . . Years later, in 1933 when Mom and Dad were married and moved into that house, they could look "unto the hills" towards Learned Plan where Mom was born and brought up . . . An interesting historical fact about this hymn: The author, Marquis of Lorne, wrote it while on a visit to the Eastern Townships and being inspired by all the beautiful hills and mountains. He later became Governor-General of Canada. (Malcolm Fraser)

View from Pine Hill Farm towards Learned Plain and Megantic Mountain, ca. 1970 (photo by author)

View from Pine Hill Farm front door toward Cookshire and the Stoke Range, ca. 1970 (photo by author)

Planting new white pine tree at Pine Hill Farm, Fraser Reunion 1998 (photo by author)

Pine Hill Farm cake at 2012 Fraser Reunion in Johnville (photo by author)

There is a humorous side note to Malcolm's participation in Church activities. He was so involved in so many aspects of Church affairs, both locally and in the Diocese, that *The Record* mistakenly identified him in a photo as "Bishop Mac Fraser." Later they issued a correction that ended his short-lived reign as Bishop!

Host Malcolm serves a scoop at 2004 Fraser Reunion (photo by author)

(Back row) Canon Curtis Patterson, Rt. Rev. Bruce Stavert, Canon Ron West and Bishop Mac Fraser. (Front row) Irene Fisher, Mary Kirby, Sheila Bellam, Laurel James, Jane Bishop and Dorothy Ross. Absent: William Lyon... historic day.

The Record's goof re "Bishop Mac Fraser" (*The Record*, March 1997)

Piper performs at Fraser Reunion at Pine Hill Farm, 2013 (photo by author)

Passing the Pitchfork

In recent years, the family farm in Canada has experienced dramatic decline due to various economic, sociological and external factors. Ever increasing government regulations and the economies of scale have placed the small family farm in a very tough position. And, several years ago, the mad cow scare dealt an enormous blow to the beef industry – a blow from which it still has not fully recovered. Pine Hill Farm was not immune to these negative conditions. The situation was exacerbated by Malcolm's deteriorating health as a result of multiple system atrophy. Hence it was not surprising that in 2010 he retired from active farming, sold his remaining livestock and shut the barn doors for good. No, it was not surprising – but it was very sad nonetheless. Doreen relates his departure from the farm he loved:

> Mac's illness ended his ability to drive. In May 2012 he became housebound and required care. On October 16, 2012, he entered long-term care at Grace Christian Home [now Grace Village] in Huntingville [Quebec]. I left the farm in June 2013 and moved to Magog to live across the road from my sister on Fitch Bay Road where I grew up – that is, I returned home! (Doreen Fraser)

Meanwhile, what became of the pitchfork? It still sits there just inside the upper barn stable door, waiting for someone to take it. Waiting . . . waiting . . . waiting. Whether someone steps forward to continue the tradition of tilling this land is an open question. For the moment, we are grateful that the farmhouse is being occupied and cared for by Marc Nault, a professor at Cégep de Sherbrooke.

Whereas the first six chapters of this book have focussed on the succession of Pine Hill Farm custodians, the next few chapters provide details of various internal and external elements closely associated with the farm.

Hoarfrost in hayloft created by hot air rising from stable below, ca. 1975 (photo by author)

Malcolm's purebred polled Herefords in pasture, ca. 1990 (photo by author)

Chapter 7
The Railways: Boom and Bust

Pine Hill Farm from CPR tracks, ca. 1957 (photo by author)

Author's note: Much of the research for this chapter was done by my brother Jim Fraser for his feature article "A Brief History of Cookshire's Railways," published in the July 2013 issue of the Fraser Family Link.

For almost 150 years, the sights and sounds of trains have penetrated the peacefulness of Pine Hill Farm. A low, deep rumble would foretell the approach of a freight train from "up the tracks." The train would emerge from the woods, whistle piercing the air, as it twisted around the bend and sped down the steep grade past the trout ponds and the level crossing at the foot of Fraser Road. Our farmhouse windows would rattle as the train passed. Then it became quiet again – until the next train came through. Such was the scene when two railways (the CPR and the Maine Central) were your next door neighbours. Over the years we saw steam locomotives, diesel engines and self-propelled Budd cars. Boxcars, flat cars, tank cars, handcars and inspection cars. Even cabooses that have long since gone the way of the dodo bird. We counted the freight cars and tried to see inside the sleeper cars. Yes, we saw it all every day but never got bored doing so. In a sense, we and the railways were one.

Railway Fever

In the middle of the 19th century, transportation in North America was by steam-powered boat or by horse-drawn wagons/coaches in summer over rough roads, or by sleighs in winter. The extensive highway network we take for granted today was non-existent – the motorcar had not yet been invented – and railways were in their infancy. However, due to recent dramatic advances in the design of steam locomotives, rail fever was starting to run rampant. Recognition of the huge potential of railways as engines (no pun intended) of economic growth and development was spurring a tremendous growth of railway networks. The new-fangled railways were an efficient, highly effective means of transporting raw materials to factories and ports, and finished goods to market. Towns fortunate enough to become served by a railway had a greatly enhanced chance of growth, economic development and prosperity. For passengers, travel by "iron horse" coach was much faster – not to mention infinitely more comfortable! As elsewhere, entrepreneurs in Quebec caught rail fever; new railway lines could not be built fast enough for their liking.

The railways of Cookshire owe their existence to one man above all others – John Henry Pope. Pope, Cookshire's most prominent citizen, wore many hats – farmer, militia volunteer, businessman, entrepreneur and politician. He served as Member of Parliament for Compton County for 22 consecutive years, from Confederation in 1867 until his death in 1889. Pope was arguably one of John A. Macdonald's most influential cabinet ministers, holding several important portfolios, notably Minister of Railways and Canals from 1885 to 1889. He saw economic opportunity in additional rail connections to Maine and the Maritimes. He envisioned a new railway from Sherbrooke, through Compton County (where it would serve his lumber and other business interests), across Maine (with its countless New England interconnections, including to the ice-free port of Portland), then on to Saint John, N.B. For passengers travelling between Montreal and the Atlantic colonies, the overnight route through Maine would be much shorter and much quicker than competing routes.

Pope's Railway

Pope's St. Francis and Megantic International Railway, later known as simply the International Railway or the Short Line, was established (i.e., chartered) in 1870. Because major challenges were encountered in raising the necessary capital, Pope invested heavily of his own money to personally finance construction, which commenced in the winter of 1871-72. On July 15, 1875, the newly completed first section, from Sherbrooke east through Cookshire to Robinson (now Bury), was inaugurated amidst great celebration. In 1879 service to Lake Megantic (as it was then called) was inaugurated. Pope's ultimate dream was finally realized in 1888, when the entire route, from Sherbrooke to Saint John, N.B., was inaugurated. The railway now stretched "from sea to sea." Unfortunately, Pope did not live long enough to witness the huge impact his railway would have on his beloved hometown and his country; his health was failing and he died the following year, in 1889 at age 69.

Steam train passing Cookshire station (Jim Shaughnessy, *The Call of Trains*)

Vintage photo of Cookshire station (author's collection)

The coming of the railway to Cookshire was met with much celebration by the people but less so by the horses. A newspaper article from 1892 documents a near-tragic instance of their discontent with this new mode of transportation:

> This Wednesday morning the double team of Mr. Alton Hodge became frightened near the station and ran away. Mr. Hodge was thrown out and badly stunned and was carried into the house of Mr. Wm. Bailey and it was found that he had two ribs broken. The horses were stopped at Frasier's crossing just in front of the train. One of the horses fell onto the track, and the engine was stopped not ten feet away. (*Compton County Chronicle*, May 11, 1892)

Team of horses startled by steam locomotive (sketch by James Harvey)

The Railways

Pine Hill Farm from CPR tracks, ca. 1980 (photo by author)

View of CPR and Maine Central Railroad tracks and Eaton River from Pine Hill Farm, ca. 1960 (photo by author)

Tough Climb

As a child, I was always impressed by the speed at which the steam locomotives passed the crossing below our farm, spewing out huge plumes of black smoke and causing the ground to shake violently. However, once the engines had disappeared from view, the train gradually lost speed as it almost slowed to a crawl. In fact, occasionally, it would grind to a dead halt. When that happened, the train would have to back up and take another run at it. I remember my dad telling me that the grade from Cookshire to Birchton was the steepest anywhere on the CPR line east of the Rockies. While that may not have been completely true, the grade was definitely significant, as indicated by this article:

> Between Sherbrooke and Lake Megantic, there were three river valleys and three summits to negotiate. The CPR determined to cross all of these at right-angles . . . From Lennoxville eastward, the 14 miles to the summit at Birchton were a steady climb on 1.4 to 1.7% grades. Down from the 974-foot height, the line descended to the valley of the Eaton River at Cookshire on a 1.3% slope . . . Crossed the Eaton River on a 210-foot deck-plate girder bridge and tackled the 9-mile climb at 1% or better to Bury. Beyond Bury, it was uphill to Gould over 4 miles to reach 1,300 feet. Over this crest, the line slid down through the woods to the Salmon River at Scotstown where, at the east end of the yard, the 1% began again. For seven miles to Milan and Spring Hill the railway continued, to the height of land between the St. Francis and Chaudiere Rivers. Spring Hill, elevation 1,690 feet, was the highest point on this subdivision. There followed eight miles of descent on 0.9 to 1.1% grades to the shore of

CPR freight train hauled by eight locomotives climbs the grade past Pine Hill Farm, 1982 (photo by author)

The Railways

Lake Megantic and Agnes, the original terminus of the railway and the beginning of the next short 16-mile stage to the International Boundary. (exporail.org)

Hereford Railway

The Pope family was also associated with Cookshire's second railway line. John Henry Pope's son-in-law, William Bullock Ives, saw business opportunities in additional railway linkages to the United States – a rapidly growing market for lumber and other raw materials. After a strike by the 1200-man construction crew that had been cheated out of their wages was quelled by the militia, the 36-mile (58-km) line was completed on January 6, 1889, connecting the CPR at Cookshire south to Hereford Township and the Upper Coos Railroad at Beecher Falls, Vt. That summer, the line was extended 13 miles (21 km) in the opposite direction, north from "Cookshire Junction" to Dudswell Junction on the Quebec Central Railway. In 1890 the Hereford Railway was leased to the Maine Central Railroad and operated as its Quebec Division. In 1925 it was acquired by the CPR.

As was the case with the International Railway, this new railway passed directly through the Pine Hill Farm property. A deed dated 1888 describes the piece of property purchased as "part of the Lots Nos. Nine and Ten in the 8th range of the said Township of Eaton."

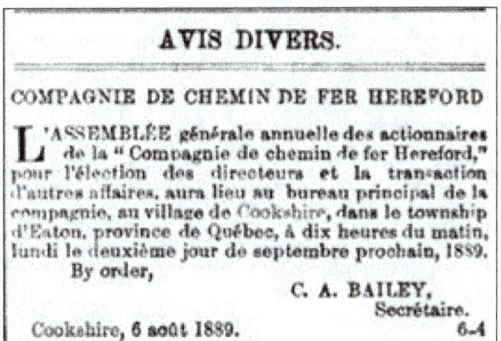

Notice of Annual Meeting of Hereford Railway Company, 1889 (*Canada Gazette*)

Official cadastral reference, Maine Central Railway [*sic*] right-of-way (registrefoncier.gouv.qc.ca)

Like many other railway short lines, the Hereford Railway was short-lived. It was abandoned in sections, starting in 1927. The final 7-mile (11-km) segment from Cookshire to Sawyerville continued to serve the sawmill in Sawyerville, with a few freight cars per week, and also served as a siding for the CPR main line until it was finally abandoned in 1977 and the tracks taken up.

Documentation of sale of Pine Hill Farm land to Hereford Railway Company, 1888 (Fraser family archives)

The Railways

Steam locomotive at Cookshire station on Maine Central Railroad track, ca. 1957 (photo by author)

View from Pine Hill Farm of trains on both CPR and Maine Central Railroad tracks, ca. 1960 (photo by author)

Products and Passengers

In its heyday the CPR mainline through Cookshire was heavily trafficked. Freight trains of often a hundred or more cars hauled pulpwood, lumber, paper, textiles and footwear, prairie wheat, and later, oil and automobiles. Over the years, the cargo also included many Cookshire-produced goods, including lumber from Ives' Cookshire Mill Co.; methanol, creosote and other wood-derived chemical products from the Standard Chemical Co. (of which John Henry Pope served as manager); patent medicines from Frasier, Thornton & Co.; wool blankets and textiles from

Cookshire Woollen Mills; silverware from Wallace Silversmiths; plastic containers from General Plastics (and its various successors); and tent trailers from Bon-Air Leisure Industries. Pine Hill Farm took direct advantage of the freight services, shipping bundles of Christmas trees and drums of late-season maple syrup.

Charles Fraser freight invoice, St. Francis and Megantic International Railway, 1876 (Fraser family archives)

CPR passenger train at Cookshire Station, 1964 (photo by author)

Cookshire was well served by passenger rail service on its CPR mainline. Two overnight trains with sleeper cars – one in each direction – linked Montreal to Saint John, N.B., and Halifax, N.S., daily. During World War II, service was doubled to four trains daily. The four-train service continued until 1955, when the steam trains were replaced by faster diesel locomotives. The new twice-daily diesel service (one train in each direction) was christened The Atlantic Limited. Twice-daily Dayliner service, using self-propelled Budd cars, was added in the late 1950s and shuttled between Montreal and Lac Mégantic.

By the 1960s, passenger rail traffic in North America was in sharp decline, due mainly to the dramatically increased popularity of automobile travel and the advent of air travel. On the CPR mainline through Cookshire, the first casualty was the Dayliner, which ceased operation in the early 1970s.

International Railway winter timetable, 1888 (*The Weekly Examiner*, May 18, 1888)

Dayliner passes Pine Hill Farm lower pasture, ca. 1962 (photo by author)

CP Rail timetable, 1972.
Above: brochure cover
Right: Montreal to Saint John, N.B. timetable
(Fraser family archives)

On December 16, 1994, Via Rail's "Atlantic" passenger train between Montreal and Halifax made its last run. Two passengers recall the experience:

> My good friend Dick James and I rode the Atlantic on its farewell voyage. It was a bittersweet trip. At each station, a small crowd of well-wishers and media gathered to witness and record history. Along the tracks, people stood and waved to their departing friend. As we passed Pine Hill Farm, Malcolm and Doreen flashed the kitchen lights repeatedly in silent tribute. (James Fraser)

Cookshire, mile 47.4, was about a mile ahead. First though would be the crossing of the Eaton River. The CPR alignment's approach to the bridge is a downhill curve. At the other end of the bridge is a reverse uphill curve. Train 41 slowed and I felt the slight jerking action of the cars as the consist rumbled over the bridge. The engineer was slowing to stop at Cookshire if necessary. The station platform was deserted and with two hoots from the front, the E8 began spewing out a steady stream of dark exhaust. The train continued its climb out of town on the Megantic Subdivision's westbound ruling grade. The only other scheduled flag-stop between Megantic and Sherbrooke had also been omitted. Cookshire is the junction station with the Sawyerville Subdivision. All the secondary tracks were void of cars, probably owing to the lack of carload shippers and consignees in Sawyerville. (extratrainstuff.blogspot.com)

CPR freight train climbs the steep grade past Pine Hill Farm, ca. 1985 (photo by author)

Very short freight train with caboose passes Pine Hill Farm ponds, 1981 (photo by author)

CPR steam locomotives pass Fraser crossing, ca. 1954 (photo by author)

The Railways

Ever since train service came to Cookshire, our family took frequent advantage of it. Dad used to tell of taking the train as a boy to visit his Uncle Hollis and other Joyce relatives out Bishopton/Dudswell way, and of going to watch baseball games in Sawyerville and hockey in Berlin, N.H. During the early 1960s, when I was studying at Bishop's University, I would often take the Dayliner from Lennoxville to Cookshire. Two of my fellow students, Jim Robinson and David Laberee, took the same train, but jumped off at the Bulwer flag stop. Once, the conductor forgot to inform the engineer, who blew straight through Bulwer without stopping! The train had almost reached Birchton when the error was realized. But no problem – the engineer sounded three long blasts of the horn to indicate reverse and then backed up, all the way back to Bulwer. Some years later, Mom and Dad took the train to Montreal to visit their newborn grandchild (my eldest daughter).

Maine Central Railroad culvert and Fraser's brook, 2019 (photo by author)

Mishaps

As with any mode of transportation, accidents sometimes happened on the railway and Cookshire was not immune. Although nothing on the scale of the apocalyptic 2013 rail disaster in Lac Mégantic – in which 47 people were killed – was experienced, there were occasionally derailments and other mishaps. My cousin Charles recounts one from the 1920s that his dad told him about:

> The story begins in Birchton, just a couple of miles above Cookshire. They were trying to move a flatcar full of railway ties. But the flatcar got away from them and started rolling down the steep grade toward Cookshire.

Because it was so heavily loaded, it picked up speed very quickly. They said that when it went by your folks' farm, it was literally whistling. At the same time, a railway crew was working with a pile driver on a bridge just beyond Cookshire. The men could hear the flatcar coming because it was making such a loud noise. Everybody was able to jump out of the way but the rocketing flatcar ran right over the pile driver car on the bridge and smashed it to smithereens. (Charles W. K. Fraser)

Birchton was also the scene of a bona fide train wreck in 1951. A double-headed freight train derailed and left two steam locomotives and several freight cars on their sides in the woods. Apparently the cause was a steam boiler had run low on water. In any case, it was the talk of the town and many, including my dad, rushed to the site to witness the spectacular scene.

Birchton train wreck, Nov. 25, 1951 (author's collection)

Although the glory days of Cookshire's railways are long past, the few remaining trains that pass by Pine Hill Farm still serve to rekindle those memories.

Chapter 8
The Sugar Bush: How Sweet it Was!

Horses and sap sled at Pine Hill Farm sugar camp, ca. 1960 (photo by author)

Of all the various farming activities at Pine Hill Farm, one stood out from all others – maple sugaring. Perhaps it was because of the season in which it occurred and the unique middle-of-the-woods environment where it took place. Or maybe it was due to the unforgettable aromas generated by the boiling process. For me, it was both of those reasons, and one more – it meant getting time off school. (I intensely disliked school!)

Sugaring was carried on every spring at Pine Hill Farm for almost a century. In early years, all the sap collected was boiled into sugar. Maple syrup and maple wax came on the scene only several decades later. (Depending upon the amount of boiling, different maple products are produced. The main ones are maple butter, maple syrup, maple wax or taffy, soft sugar and hard maple sugar.) These products represented a very important cash crop that was sold outright or bartered in exchange for other goods. The following table shows the price evolution of maple sugar and syrup over the century of operation.

Evolution of Maple Prices, 1875–1965

Year	Sugar	Syrup
1875	$0.10 /lb.	
1878	$0.09 /lb.	
1879	$0.08 /lb.	
1897	$0.07 /lb.	
1899	$0.05 /lb.	
1908	$0.06 /lb.	
1909	$0.07 /lb.	
1911	$0.07 /lb.	
1912	$0.07 /lb.	
1912	$0.08 /lb.	
1918		$1.60 /gal.
1920		$2.75 /gal.
1957		$5.00 /gal.
1958		$5.50 /gal.
1965		$5.50 /gal.

(data from Fraser family archives)

Abenaki Discovery

From the late 1800s, maple sugaring has been an important part of Pine Hill Farm's operations. But the maple sugar industry is centuries older than that. Long before the European explorers "discovered" the New World, the Abenaki First Nations people had discovered the miracle of the maple tree. They found that, in early spring, by cutting a gash in the tree's trunk, they could obtain a sweet water-like liquid. After sufficient boiling, they found that it would yield sugar. According to early missionaries, maple sugar was a mainstay of the Abenaki diet. The white settlers wasted little time in adopting this springtime activity.

Abenakis making maple sugar (Bea Nelson, sokokisojourn.wordpress.com)

The Sugar Camp

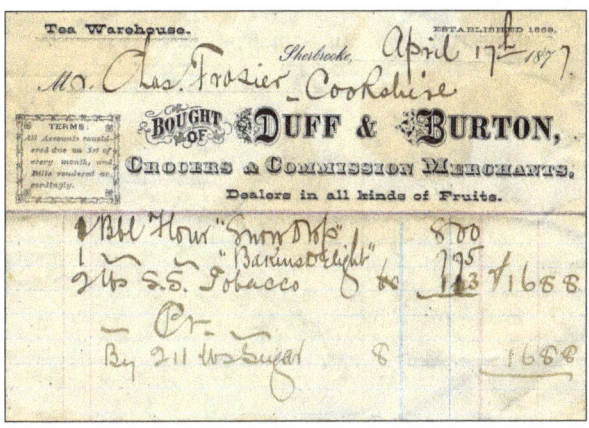

Duff and Burton invoice paid by maple sugar, 1877 (Fraser family archives)

It is believed that it was my grandfather, Charles Ira Fraser, who built the sugar camp and began sugaring at Pine Hill Farm. In an interview with the *Sherbrooke Record* in 1965, my dad told the reporter that the building was constructed around 1890. But newly discovered family records indicate that maple sugar was being made on the farm as early as 1877. An invoice from Duff and Burton dated April 17, 1877, shows that purchased goods were paid for "by 211 lbs [maple] sugar."

The sugar camp building – still standing today – is described as follows in a 1904 insurance policy: "A frame shingle-roofed building, used as a Sugar Camp 20 ft x 30 ft with addition 12 ft x 18 ft." The addition referred to is what we called the "tank

Grimm Mfg. Co. invoice for maple sugaring supplies, 1917 (Fraser family archives)

house." It housed a 1418-gallon (6446-litre) zinc-lined reservoir to store the sap while waiting to be boiled.

In the earliest years, the maple production records were inscribed on the walls and doorposts of the sugar camp. More recently, it was my mom's daily diaries that kept track of these statistics. The following table, compiled from those diary entries by my brother Warren, covers the period from 1949 to 1969 – the last years that sugaring was carried on at Pine Hill Farm.

The summary table shows that the 1954 sugaring season was by far the longest, at a whopping 49 days. But that does not tell the whole story. In fact, a good first run at the beginning of March was followed by a very cold spell that lasted three full weeks during which the sap did not run a drop! There were times when the sap ran in a stream, the buckets overflowed and

Pine Hill Farm Sugaring Statistics, 1949–1969

Year	Start date	End date	Duration (days)	No. of taps	Syrup (gal.)
1949	Mar. 28	Apr. 18	21	–	–
1950	Apr. 1	Apr. 27	27	450	–
1951	Mar. 20	Apr. 10	21	450	–
1952	Mar. 27	Apr. 19	23	650	–
1953	Mar. 20	Apr. 9	20	–	–
1954	Mar. 2	Apr. 20	49	750	–
1955	–	Apr. 22	–	–	–
1956	Apr. 2	May 1	30	–	–
1957	Mar. 16	Apr. 20	35	750	–
1958	–	–	–	–	–
1959	–	–	–	–	–
1960	Apr. 2	Apr. 22	20	725	–
1961	Mar. 25	Apr. 21	27	660	160
1962	Mar. 22	Apr. 27	36	–	198
1963	Apr. 4	Apr. 26	23	–	130
1964	Mar. 23	Apr. 22	31	–	105
1965	Apr. 5	Apr. 29	25	825	130
1966	Mar. 21	Apr. 23	33	–	195
1967	Mar. 27	Apr. 17+	21+	700	120+
1968	Mar. 26	Apr. 13	19	736	158
1969	Apr. 7	Apr. 24	18	–	84

Note: – indicates missing data; 1 gal. = 4.55 litres. (data from Alice Fraser's diaries, compiled by Warren Fraser)

the tank house reservoir was full to the top. The week of April 2-8, 1966, must have been one of those times. By Mom's account, Dad made a total of 101 gallons (459 litres) of syrup in that one week alone, including an incredible 27 gallons (123 litres) on April 4: "Dad boiled until midnight – 27 gals." Sugaring at Pine Hill Farm was very much a family affair. Mom meticulously recorded the daily participation of the family workforce in different ways including scattering buckets, tapping, putting up the stovepipes, cleaning the pans, levelling the arch, gathering, boiling, picking up the buckets, washing the buckets, cleaning the pans (again) and taking down the stovepipes.

The Sugar Bush

Typical Learned & Taylor debit-credit account statement, including purchase of a new sugaring pan (indicated by dashed red line), 1879 (Fraser family archives)

Late start danger to ET sugar season

By PAUL WHITELAW
(Record Staff Reporter)

Smoke rose from sugar camps all over the Eastern Townships yesterday as maple sap trickled into galvanized buckets and farmers with horses and tractors started collecting and cooking their 1965 crop of maple syrup.

The producers of the major share of the world's maple sugar crop, district sugar bush operators reported sap was flowing for the first time this season in all sections of the Eastern Townships.

Following a very early start by some operators during the first days of March, operations later were frozen solid. Sap didn't start flowing again until Sunday afternoon and didn't really start flowing again well until yesterday, sugar bush operators reported.

With the season only a few days old, the farmers report that the outlook is still very uncertain.

Most farmers questioned by the Record said the late starting date this year (the season is usually in full swing around March 15) will probably mean a shorter season and a smaller crop.

OLD OAKEN, PLASTIC, AND GALVANIZED BUCKETS — Cookshire farmer Donald Fraser says he started sugaring in 1911 with oaken buckets. He later converted to galvanized buckets and recently tried plastic buckets and bags, although he is not pleased with the results. "The sap has a plastic taste," he says.

Donald Fraser in maple sugaring article (*Sherbrooke Daily Record*, Apr. 7, 1965)

The combined efforts of the conscripted family workforce was not always sufficient to meet the labour needs. This resulted in the occasional hiring of outside help, mainly for boiling. Among those documented in Mom's daily writings are "Mr. Boleo" (i.e., neighbour Louis Beaulieu), Clement Flaws, Jim French, Alden Learned and Tom Migneault. An eclectic cast of volunteers supplemented the regular workforce, sometimes for specialized tasks, but often just to help out with the regular activities. Among those earning at least a mention were Cousin Cecil Gilbert, Alec and Sandy Booth, Howard Barter, Ernie Cork, Cousin Oscar Joyce and "Mr. Smith."

Sugaring involved various challenges, some related to the weather, others related to the sugaring equipment. Mom's diary entry for March 16, 1957, is quite unique: "Dad and boys cleaned up tank, fixed bullet hole." Trudging through knee-deep snow carrying two heavy pails of sap was no easy job. But gathering frozen sap was even harder – and sometimes impossible. It involved punching a hole through the ice in the bucket to access the small amount of liquid sap under it. The diary entries for April 5 and 6, 1963, illustrate this situation: (April 5) "Boys tried to gather and boil, no luck, frozen solid." (April 6) "Boys gathered tub of frozen sap in p.m."

The last runs of the season resulted in "buddy" syrup that was poured into heavy steel drums and taken to Casavants for shipping to Beauce where it was used in chewing tobacco and in medicines. Typical diary references are those of April 28, 1950: "Dad boiled in all the sap; 5 gal. of dark buddy syrup." and April 28, 1954: "Took syrup in drums to Casavants." In later years, "buddy" syrup was shipped by truck to the maple syrup producers' cooperative in Plessisville.

Donald Fraser stoking fire in Pine Hill Farm maple sap evaporator, ca. 1962 (photo by author)

Statement of revenue for maple syrup in drums, 1965 (Fraser family archives)

Dad last sugared in 1969. The bush of approximately 1000 maples has lain dormant ever since. Well, almost dormant. In April 1988, for old time sake, I decided to do a mini-sugaring. I wanted to once more experience the sweet aroma of boiling sap in the spring sunshine. So I packed up the family, including my mother-in-law, and the necessary supplies (bitstock for tapping and buckets for collecting) and headed to Cookshire, about a three-hour drive from our home in Rosemere, north of Montreal. As soon as we arrived, we trekked through the snow to the sugar camp about a mile away. Fortunately, the weather was perfect and the sap began to run as soon as we tapped the dozen trees close by. Within an hour there was enough sap to begin boiling it in the large metal caldron we placed outdoors over an open fire. By the end of the day we had made about two quarts of maple syrup. It was an experience I will cherish forever.

Through the years, my brother Malcolm and I have toyed with idea of together doing a full-blown sugaring operation. The plan was that I would take two weeks of my annual vacation and come out to the Townships to help him. Unfortunately it never happened. One of the problems was that it was impossible to plan ahead due to the unpredictability of the sugar season start date. Malcolm refers to this in a letter to me dated March 17, 1987:

> It's been snowy and blustery here today and yesterday. No sugaring yet – I guess it's waiting for your holidays. There is talk of [the syrup price] around $40 per gallon this year. If we made 150 gallons, that would be $6000 – just like that! Oh well, I wouldn't know what to do with that kind of money! (Malcolm Fraser)

Changing Methods

Over time, traditional maple sugaring methods have been replaced by successively more sophisticated ones. Tapping, collecting, and processing have all seen significant changes.

The tool used to "tap" the maple tree evolved from an axe to a hand auger to a battery-powered drill. Dad used a manual bitstock and drill.

A similar progression has occurred with respect to the container to collect the sap. The hollowed log was replaced by a succession of manufactured buckets: first wooden, then tin, followed by galvanized steel

Vintage wooden sap bucket and spout (photo by author)

The Sugar Bush

Author's family making maple syrup the old-fashioned way in Pine Hill Farm sugar bush, 1988 (photos by author)

and plastic, which was introduced in the early 1960s. (Later in the 1960s, the container was eliminated completely and replaced by a system of plastic tubing connecting the trees directly to the sugar camp.) Dad agreed to try both a plastic bucket and a plastic bag but never bought any more of either, preferring to stick with the galvanized bucket. He claimed that they made the sap taste "plasticky." In retrospect, he could be called one of the earliest anti-plastic crusaders.

Originally, the sap was gathered by men on snowshoes carrying two large pails suspended from a wooden neck yoke. Later, oxen or draft horses were used to haul a wooden sled bearing a bulky wooden barrel. More recently, tractors with galvanized tanks replaced the animal-drawn apparatus. Finally, with the introduction of the plastic pipeline system, the need to gather the sap was completely eliminated.

Through the years, the main processing equipment – the evaporator – was also being upgraded for more efficient boiling. My mom's diary notes one such upgrade: "1952 Feb. 28: New sugar rig."

More Than Money

Maple sugaring was one of those agricultural operations where the pleasure outweighed the profitability. The 1960s syrup selling price of $5 a gallon (equivalent to $1.10 per litre) certainly left little, if any, real profit. But that didn't seem to matter, as expressed in the lyrics of a song by singer/songwriter (and former schoolmate) Jim Robinson, whose dad was also a sugar maker in nearby Bulwer. The first verse goes like this:

> i said dad we're making maple syrup again
> barely covering costs
> son you're right i haven't added things up
> the weatherman says there'll be frost
> but hey i'm glad you mentioned it
> all this hard work for nothing's no joke
> & if i was depending on sugaring for a living
> you're right i'd be broke. (Jim Robinson)

Sweet Memories

Maple sugaring was always more than a farming activity. At the turn of the 19th century, a "sugaring off" was a major social occasion. Dressed in their best Sunday attire, scores of invited guests would make their way through snowdrifts and open water-holes to the sugar camp in the middle of the forest. The entire crowd would pose for a group photograph using the sugar camp as a backdrop. Food, fellowship and, of course, fresh maple sugar served on wooden paddles made this an unforgettable experience for all.

The Sugar Bush

Sugaring off at Pine Hill Farm sugar camp, ca. 1895 (Fraser family archives)

Local newspapers of the period frequently reported maple-sugaring related events. Some examples:

> Last week was fine for sugar makers, with the exception that they complain they had to work too hard to save their sap. A very large quantity of fine sugar was made, however, that will compensate them for their labour and loss of sleep, as many had to work night and day. All the friends have been busy also attending the various sugar orchards at the invitations of the proprietors, eating warm sugar and having good times. (*Compton County Chronicle*, Apr. 27, 1892)

The WCTU [Women's Christian Temperance Union] meeting enjoyed wax and dumplings. (*Compton County Chronicle*, Apr. 27, 1892)

5/ STUFF LIKE THAT 4:53

i said dad we're making maple syrup again
barely covering costs
son you're right i haven't added things up
the weatherman says there'll be frost
but hey i'm glad you mentioned it
all this hard work for nothing's no joke
& if i was depending on sugaring for a living
you're right i'd be broke

but driving a team of horses
decked out with a full set of bells
heart keeping time with the dripping of the sap in the pails
heading for the camp sailing up the ramp
holding on to your hat
how do you put a price on stuff like that

years rolled by & i'd left home
when dad cut the farm in two
sold the part below the road
with the barn the fields & the view
up until the day he died he'd say
i'd rather boil than eat & laugh
& he kept the woods & he kept on sugaring
never did do the math

driving a team of horses....

drove out by the old farm yesterday
thinking the sap would be running a stream
no horses no bells no buckets any more
but last night in my dream
hey son you're making music again not even covering costs
i said dad you're right i haven't added things up
but the next one's going to take off

driving a team of horses....

driving a team of horses....
how do you put a price on stuff like that
how do you put a price on stuff like that

Lyrics to "Stuff Like That," a song about maple sugaring (Jim Robinson)

Emptying load of sap at sugar camp, ca. 1965 (photo by author)

Some of the many carvings and inscriptions on the walls of Pine Hill Farm's sugar camp (photos by author or David Fraser)

On Wednesday evening, April 20, Cookshire Concert Band entertained at a very delightful sugar social and informal dance in the band room. A few well rendered selections of band music opened the evening, after which an orchestra furnished music for the dancing. Refreshments, including sugar on snow, were served in a well-organized manner at eleven o'clock. Another hour of dancing brought to a close a most enjoyable social evening. (*Sherbrooke Daily Record*, Apr. 27, 1932)

Even today, for most Quebecers, spring is not spring if you don't make at least one visit to a maple sugar bush. They are attracted by those special sights, sounds and smells – the sight of billowing white clouds of steam escaping through the cupola of the picturesque sugar shack, the drip...drip...drip sound of sap running into a galvanized bucket and the heavenly smell of freshly made maple syrup. And who can forget the taste of "sugar-on-snow," or "tire" as it is known in French – that delicious result of pouring hot syrup onto a trough of ice-cold snow?

Everyone who has ever participated in or observed maple sugaring retains fond memories of their experience. Below is a sampling of such recollections, including several by my siblings who shared their memories in issues of the Fraser Family Link:

Wooden sculpture of farmer gathering sap, Cabane à sucre Constantin, Saint-Eustache, Que. (photo by author)

> As a young teen, I loved the sugar season, especially driving the team of horses gathering the sap and enjoying the great aroma of boiling sap coming from the sugar camp. (Stevens Fraser)
>
> I remember drinking sap from the buckets early in the sugaring season . . . also taking sips of Dad's warm maple syrup from the dipper. (Karen Fraser Jackson)
>
> The smells were good and I enjoyed watching Dad stoke the fire. When there were just coals left, it was time to get out the little frying pan with the long handle and fry some eggs – they were the best ever! I once took a paddle and scraped some syrup off the felt strainer, full of nitre – it worked faster than castor oil! (June Fraser Patterson)

View of Pine Hill Farm from edge of woods, ca. 1960 (photo by author)

I remember the wonderful treat of being able to fry an egg in a little bit of syrup, through the door in the arch – it was DEE-LIC-IOUS! (John "Jack" Fraser)

How did you make out at Sugaring this spring? Did you make much Sugar and Honey? It makes my mouth water to think about it, believe me! (Frank Brennan, former hired hand)

I remember the steamy warmth of the sugar camp, the air thick with the sweet smell of boiling sap and feeling privileged to be helping Dad boil instead of gathering the sap like my brothers. (James Fraser)

I recall the sweet smell inside the camp and the thrill of riding on the sap sled as the horses raced across the bridge over the brook. (David Fraser)

My favourite time to visit the farm was during sugaring season. If I arrived at the right time, I sometimes got lucky and managed to hitch a sleigh ride with you folks to the sugar camp where your dad always made sure to give us visitors a sweet treat of the maple syrup that he was preparing. I remember helping to collect sap from the buckets. Sometimes there was still quite a lot of snow on the ground. I would arrive home tired but happy. I loved it in the woods. (Dorothy Shelton Dionne)

In the 1930s and 1940s, Mom and I used to make a trek every spring to Uncle Donald's sugar bush. I helped her carry home that 20-lb. Domestic Shortening pail of maple syrup – it was a long 2½-mile walk for my little short legs. I also remember that Charlie Fraser installed a phone line from the house to the sugar camp so that Uncle Donald and Aunt Alice could keep in touch during the day. (Carl Jackson)

Lots of sugaring memories: the cool of spring and the heat in the shack, the beautiful smells of the fire and the syrup, the taste of sap, the horses gathering, and Uncle Donald boiling. (Charles W. K. Fraser)

I remember visiting the Fraser sugar cabin and the clouds of lovely sweet steam. (Muriel French Fitzsimmons)

I fondly remember leaving the farm house with Steve, Warren, David and Jimmy; we'd cross that little wooden bridge over the stream and go up the open field into the woods with your dad driving the two horses. We'd collect the sap buckets and fill up the tank on the sleigh, then on to the sugar camp and unload. I used to love being up on the woodpile in the steam coming off the evaporator. I can smell the sweetness now. I was amazed at the piece of pork that was hung on the side of the evaporator that would, when the sap started to boil too high, reduce the boiling so it wouldn't boil over. I think it was David who would have a small frypan and take a bit of "sweet" (beyond sap but not yet syrup) with a cup; he'd open the firebox and crack a couple of farm-fresh eggs into the pan in that sweet and fry them up. I think we had these with your mom's homemade brown bread. (My sister Gail referred to this, what I called bread, as Johnny cake.) I remember it as probably having All-Bran cereal in it, sweetened with maple syrup – delicious! Your dad would always at some point call your mom on the camp phone (I think it had to be cranked first). On one occasion, if not more, on the way back to the farm in the twilight, the horses were stopped and one of them lifted its tail to relieve itself. Your dad turned around and asked me "Have you ever seen a rosebud like that?" I thought it was hilarious. I helped out on more than one occasion up at the sugar camp and absolutely loved it. Great memories! (Almon Pope)

Maple syrup display at Cookshire Fair (photo by author)

The sugar camp phone (photo by Jim Fraser)

Among my own memories of sugaring time:
- the sugaring-off process that was very exciting but extremely dangerous with the open fire exposed
- the chunks of fat pork hanging over the evaporator to keep the sap from boiling over
- finding surprises in the buckets while gathering (e.g., squirrels, mice and every species of insect)
- during a big run, staying at the camp all night to help Dad boil it down
- the old crank-operated telephone that connected the camp to the farmhouse via a single wire telephone line
- Dad's sculptured wooden neck yoke that he used when gathering
- the time the horses escaped back home, dragging a load of sap behind them
- the antique wooden paddles that hung on the walls – relics from past sugaring-offs
- the multitude of pencilled and carved inscriptions on the walls and doorposts of the sugar camp

More Than Maple

Maple products were the sweetest but not the only marketable products of the Pine Hill Farm forests. As kids, every Saturday in winter, my brothers and I would dutifully accompany Dad to the woods to selectively harvest mature spruce, fir

Malcolm Fraser cutting logs with chainsaw, ca. 1960 (photo by author)

Donald Fraser hauling logs with double sled, ca. 1950 (Fraser family archives)

and hemlock suitable to be sold to the local sawmill. (Dad didn't believe in clearcutting.) We had four tools at our disposal: the crosscut saw, the axe, the wedge and the cant dog. Our Belgian workhorse team pulled the double-runnered logging sled, and one of them, Skip, also yarded the logs. When darkness began to envelop the forest, we would head for home, with Dad piloting and Brother Malcolm riding the brake as we descended the steep hill to the farmstead. As much as I loved sugaring in the spring, I equally disliked logging in the winter – mainly because my feet and hands were always frozen due to inadequate footwear and mitts. Obviously, I much more enjoyed those occasional Saturdays when I was allowed to go play hockey with the school team!

A second cash crop that came from our woods was Christmas trees. Every fall, my Uncle Percy (Jackson) and his crew would spend several days selecting, cutting and bundling

Yarded spruce logs in Pine Hill Farm woods, ca. 1965 (photo by author)

young evergreens suitable for the American yule market. Then my dad would haul them down from the woods and stack them for transport to the Cookshire train station. In 1958, Dad received 70 cents a bunch for the trees – which worked out to approximately 10-15 cents per tree.

The maple sugar bush and the spruce forest of Pine Hill Farm were enchanting environments, each in their own way. Listening to the sap going drip-drip-drip in the warm spring sunshine was magical. Walking among the snow-laden evergreens after a winter blizzard was an exhilarating experience. Although we worked hard in both these wooded areas of the farm, the peacefulness they provided was priceless.

Revenue from sale of logs to Roy Lake's Mill, 1955 (Fraser family archives)

Christmas tree harvest, ca. 1960 (photo by author)

View of Pine Hill Farm from edge of woods, ca. 1960 (photo by author)

Returning home late Saturday afternoon with pulpwood, ca. 1958 (photo by author)

Chapter 9
Cookshire Fair : Farmers' Wares and Ferris Wheels

Draft teams, Main Building and Ferris wheel, Cookshire Fair, ca. 1985 (photo by author)

Cookshire Fair has been around since Adam was a boy. Well, not quite, but it's been happening longer than any living *homo sapiens* can remember. Residents of Cookshire and vicinity would be forgiven if they believed that it was the Frasers of Pine Hill fame who first organized the event, so closely have they been linked to its history. For more than 125 years, the folks of Pine Hill have been associated with the Fair. The first recorded Fraser involvement was in 1886 when the *Weekly*

Vintage 1897 Cookshire Fair poster (courtesy of Neil Burns)

Cookshire Fair

Examiner of July 16 reported that my grandfather, Charles Fraser, was appointed a horse judge.

Since its origin in 1845, the annual Compton County Fair has been held at a number of different venues including various Cookshire sites, Eaton Corner, Bury and Scotstown before coming to roost at its current location in Cookshire. It is interesting to note also that, in its early years, it sometimes was held in midweek instead of on a weekend.

Ad for Cookshire Fair 1892 (*Compton County Chronicle*, Sep. 7, 1892)

Long-time exhibitor and director, Walter Hodgman, shared some of the early history of the Fair at a 1985 meeting of the Bulwer sector of the Quebec Farmers Association:

> It has been held for 143 years and has been held in its present location since 1921 when stocks were sold to establish the buildings and buy the land. The first Fair Grounds were at Eaton Corner, moving to Wesleyville in 1890 where it was held for a few years. Walter exhibited there in 1900 and at Cookshire at its first fair in 1921. (*The Record*, July 5, 1985)

Cookshire Fair ca. 1900, Wesleyville Road (photo courtesy of Barb Ward)

> The directors of the Compton County Agricultural Society met at Compton Centre, March 16, for the purpose of arranging list of premiums, &c., for the Fall Fair.

Compton County Agricultural Society reference (*New England Farmer*, 1867)

Compton County Co-Operative Fair Association share certificate, 1922 (Fraser family archives)

Compton County Agricultural Society directors, ca. 1965 (courtesy of Neil Burns)

Cookshire Fair

Multiple Identities

Over the years, the event has been known by a number of different names, including:
- Compton County Agricultural Society Fall Fair (1867)
- Compton County Agricultural Society Show (1886)
- Cookshire Exhibition and Races (1892)
- St. Francis Livestock Association Fair (1897)
- Compton County Fair (1931)
- Compton County Agricultural Fair
- Cookshire Fair
- Expo Cookshire

Also, a variety of different groups have organized the Fair:
- The St-Francis Livestock Association
- Compton County Co-Operative Fair Association
- Compton County Agricultural Society (and CCAS No. 1 and CCAS No.2)

Facilities and Features

The fairground facilities have undergone many transformations over the Fair's long history. The cattle sheds that once lined the perimeter of the grounds were replaced by larger barns and a modern milking parlour. The horse sheds gave way to large dome-shaped barns made of corrugated steel. The dirt racetrack

Main Building at Cookshire Fair, ca. 2010 (photo by author)

disappeared more than 50 years ago. The iconic Main Building, built in 1938, still stands, although not in its original location, having been moved in the early 1970s when the highway was widened. The original grandstand collapsed in the winter of 1995, and a beautiful new one was built in 1995-1996. The new structure is among the finest of its kind, featuring very comfortable seat backs and lots of leg room.

In addition to the traditional rides and games, Cookshire Fair has been characterized by a wide variety of special attractions. Among the most popular were circus acts, up-and-coming young musicians (as well as some down-and-gone old musicians), and horse-pulling, tractor-pulling and truck-pulling competitions. For many years, Gastoni Attractions of Beauce operated the midway. And, of course, being an agricultural exhibition, farm equipment dealers

Compton County Fair ad (*Sherbrooke Daily Record*, Aug. 18, 1931)

Demolition of old grandstand, 1995 (photo by author)

Construction of new grandstand, 1995 (photo by author)

Farm equipment display at Cookshire Fair (photo by author)

Noël Landry Holsteins in cattle parade, Cookshire Fair, ca. 1975 (photo by author)

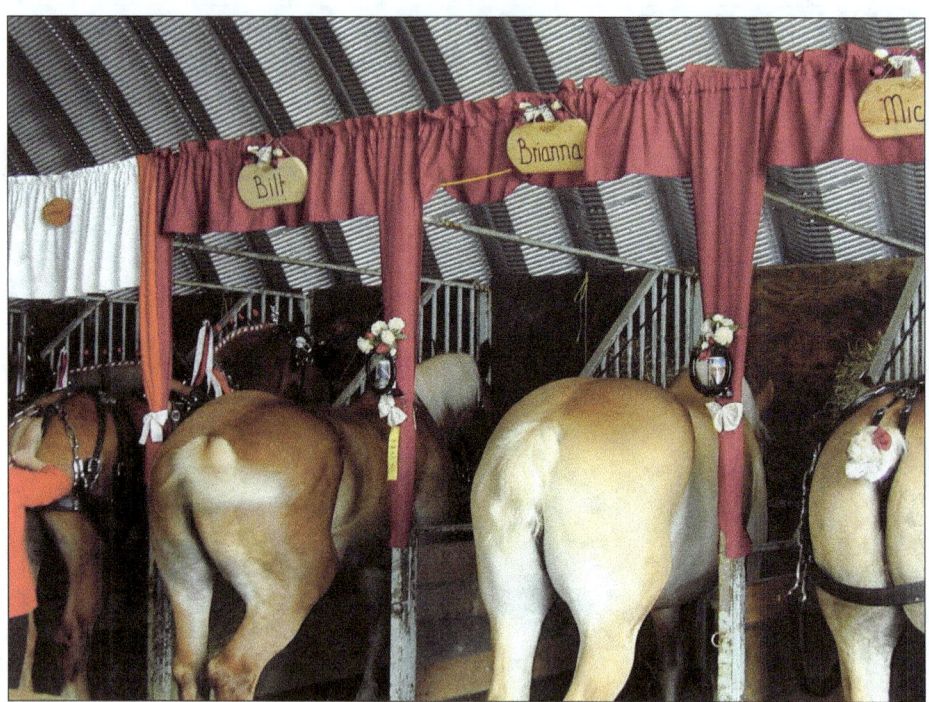
Draft horses in new horse barn, ca. 2010 (photo by author)

proudly displayed their latest models of everything from bale throwers to log splitters.

For many years, up until the 1960s, horse racing was a popular feature of the Fair. Seated very low in their sulkies and staring directly into their horses' rear ends, the fearless drivers would charge around the dusty (or muddy) half-mile track as the race announcer's play-by-play commentary blared over the crackling loudspeakers. It was very exciting because you never knew which horse would win. But back in the 1950s, you could always be sure of one thing – Bill Lancaster's nag would come in dead last! I used to feel sorry for the Lancasters, but alas, I didn't need to. Many years later, I learned that the younger generation of Lancasters were enjoying great horse racing success in the United States. And to think that it all started at Cookshire Fair!

Donald Fraser the Exhibitor

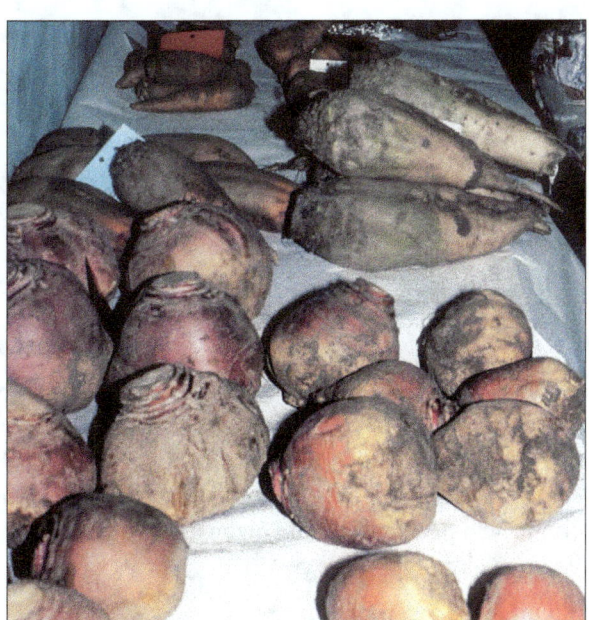

Turnips and mangles exhibits at Cookshire Fair, ca. 1970 (photo by author)

My dad was one of the premier exhibitors at the Fair. Although he was best known for his vegetables – especially turnips – he also exhibited apples, grain, maple products, ducks and pigeons. Despite the strong competition, he regularly won a good share of those coveted red First Prize cards, as indicated in *The Record's* annual list of prizewinners. Exhibitors also received cash prizes based on their standing in the different categories. In 1960, my dad's total prize money was $29.80. That same year, he also exhibited at the much larger Sherbrooke Fair where – you guessed it – he won first prize on his turnips!

- Yellow onions: 1st D. A. Fraser (*La Tribune*, Sep. 26, 1922)
- Summer cabbage: 1st Donald Fraser; Sweet corn: 1st Donald Fraser; Salsify: 1st Donald Fraser (*Sherbrooke Daily Record*, Sep. 8, 1956)

Pine Hill Farm

- Turnips: 1st Donald Fraser; Swede turnips: 1st Donald Fraser (*Sherbrooke Daily Record*, Aug. 31, 1965)
- Pumpkins, sugar: 1st Donald Fraser; Tomatoes – 3 varieties: 1st Donald Fraser (*Sherbrooke Record*, Aug. 19, 1970)

Details of Donald Fraser's Cookshire Fair prize money, 1960 (courtesy of Neil Burns)

In honour of our dad's long-time participation in the Fair as an exhibitor, some of my siblings and I established a special memorial prize awarded annually in his name for the highest aggregate in the Vegetables class.

Interestingly enough, my dad wasn't the only member of his family to show vegetables at the Fair. His younger brother Kenneth, who would later become a regular sponsor of the Fair, was among the prizewinners listed in 1928.

Donald Fraser Memorial prize (photo by author)

- Vegetables: G. Picard, Birchton; Mrs. H. A. Stevenson, Cookshire; Mrs. Walter Edwards, Cookshire; Mrs. T. O. Farnsworth, Cookshire; Guy Chaddock, Birchton; Kenneth Frasier, Cookshire (*Sherbrooke Daily Record*, Aug. 16, 1928)

Draft horse teams parade in front of grandstand, ca. 1980 (photo by author)

Horse racing at Cookshire Fair, ca. 1957 (photo by author)

And, of course, we must not forget Uncle Ken's wife, Aunt Susie, who exhibited her amazing needlework creations at the Cookshire Fair for 67 consecutive years beginning in 1936.

Even though my dad was the official exhibitor, in later years my mom assumed responsibility for Pine Hill Farm maple products: syrup, soft sugar, hard sugar and wax. The Fair was always very much a family affair, as indicated in the following recollections of my siblings, extracted from the August 1995 issue of the Fraser Family Link:

Pine Hill Farm

- Marina: . . . showing calves when I was a member of the Calf Club . . . helping Dad choose the vegetables to display
- June: . . . the general grubbiness of the midway workers and being warned not to eat any food from their booths . . . helping Dad select and place vegetables
- John: . . . the urgency of getting haying finished so we could go to the Fair . . . climbing on the new tractors and wondering whether we'd ever be able to own one at Pine Hill Farm
- Malcolm: (Too busy organizing this year's Fair to think about past ones!)
- Marilyn: . . . going to the Fair was our reward for "being good" all year. . . anxiously looking for and finding Dad's name on the red 1st prize cards
- Steve: . . . inviting a pretty young lady to go on a ride on the midway. . .
- Warren: . . . helping Dad assemble his vegetables and fruit . . . Art Bennett proclaiming the Fair to be "bigger and better than ever!" . . . cotton candy, clowns and games of chance
- Karen: . . . admiring all the exhibits and looking for Dad's red cards . . . going on the rides . . . seeing friends
- Diane: . . . serving meals in the Dining Hall . . . visiting the cattle barns and the great looking animals . . . "Win a prize every time" games . . . unexpectedly encountering a bull when taking a shortcut to the

Taking Dad's poultry exhibits to Cookshire Fair (sketch by James Harvey)

- David: . . . helping Dad select and clean the produce . . . searching for plums without wormholes . . . coming up with something original for Mom's maple products display . . . grandstand attractions, Gilbert's hotdogs, throwing darts

- James: . . . time off from haying . . . spending all day Thursday helping Dad prepare entries . . . ski-doos, evaporators and Sawyerville Baptists displays downstairs in the Main Building . . . the grubby ride operators . . . being amazed that farmers slept overnight in the cattle barns

- Cousin Charles: . . . Uncle Donald's prize turnips . . . Charlie Taylor's race horses . . . the music of the merry-go-round

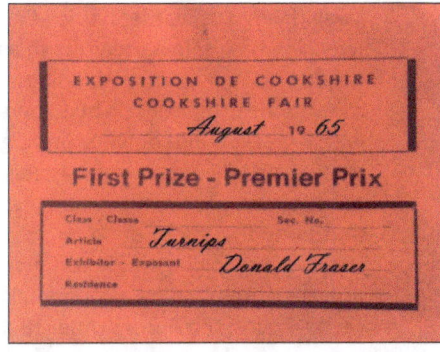

First prize ticket for turnips, 1965 (photo illustration by Marilyn Reed and author)

Malcolm the Organizer

The Fraser name – in the person of Malcolm "Mac" Fraser – is also inextricably linked to the organization of Cookshire Fair. After an early introduction to the Compton County Agricultural Society by his mentor and friend, Don MacMillan, Malcolm joined their Board of Directors and began a half-century of service that only ended due to illness. In a (Sherbrooke) *Record* article published in 2011, reporter Claudia Villemaire describes interviewing Mac at the fairgrounds:

Malcolm Fraser at work in Fair office, ca. 2010 (photo by author)

He chose the fairgrounds for the interview, and that's where we found him, his aged pickup parked in its usual place and Fraser in his usual chair [in the Fair Office], glasses on the end of his nose, cap on the table. But this day, no rubber boots... [Sometimes] we have found him shovel in hand, digging small trenches to direct water away from the cattle barns. Other times, armed with a hammer or wrecking bar, helping tear down a building on the Cookshire fairgrounds, helping to construct such things as the [new] grandstand, a collapsed roof on a cattle barn, or building a new extension to one of the stables. We've tracked him down scurrying across the grounds, taking up a stand to direct traffic while a volunteer takes a break. Years ago, when water volume couldn't meet demand, organizing water trucks and holding tanks were just a prelude to preparing facts and figures for new water sources and piping, washroom facilities and such, helping in the long process of re-building a county fair that was on the brink of closing in the early 1980s. (*The Record*, Aug. 18, 2011)

In the same interview, Malcolm reminisces and speaks about how he first got involved with the Fair:

"We always loved the fair. I remember the stories about the first exhibitions when often they were at the beginning of the week. Some years the fairgrounds were at the other end of town, other years closer to Birchton, but my family has been coming here to this spot for at least three generations," he says, adding he couldn't remember his first visits to his beloved county fair. "We were never great exhibitors [of livestock]," he admits, "although I did join the Calf Club and 4-H, and yes, I did exhibit a few times but we simply loved the fair and it didn't take long before I was coming out, offering to help out – you know. And, of course, the directors soon caught on to that and persuaded me to join their ranks and 'step up to the plate' so to speak," he says, laughing at those long ago years. (*The Record*, Aug. 18, 2011)

Malcolm was always so present at all Fair-related activities that, when he had to leave, it created a deep void, as expressed in the following newspaper article:

Cattle judging in front of new grandstand, Cookshire Fair, ca. 2000 (photo by author)

COOKSHIRE FAIR FUNDRAISING LUNCH: On Tuesday, March 12, the Cookshire Fair Board held its annual fundraising lunch and afternoon of cards at the Bury Community Center. Everyone started arriving and before long included over 60 – all awaiting a lunch of soups, sandwiches and other goodies. Before the lunch, Erwin Watson, Master of Ceremonies for the event, welcomed everyone to the lunch. After everyone's appetite was filled from the homemade soups and sweets, it was time for the many drawings and the cards to begin. There was only one thing missing from the day and that was Mac Fraser. Mac used to meet the crowd at the door of this event for many years and he wasn't able to be there this year. A while back he took sick and is now residing at a retirement home in Huntingville, Que. It felt strange not to see his grin and he was very missed. (*Colebrook Chronicle*, Mar. 22, 2013)

Cookshire Fair promo licence plate (courtesy of Kerri Fraser)

In 2013, in recognition of his long and dedicated service to the Cookshire Fair and the Eastern Townships County Fairs Association, Mac was presented with the Canadian Association of Fairs and Exhibitions volunteering award. An excerpt from the citation reads as follows:

Joining the Fair board in the mid 1960's, [Mac] quickly gained the respect of his fellow board members with his enthusiasm and sharp wit, while never losing sight of the seriousness of running a country fair. His devotion to the fair led him to serve as President for five terms and then as treasurer from 2001 to 2012. For many years, community members joked about whether Mac lived at home or at the fairgrounds because more often than not, following his retirement from Canada Post, it would be easier to find Mac at the Fair [grounds]. . . An example of his selfless desire to assist others was when he wanted

Malcolm's 60th Birthday Party invitation (Fraser family archives)

to mark a personal milestone. He organized his own 60th birthday party but asked all who attended to place a monetary donation in one of three boxes instead of bringing gifts for him. Through this generous act, he raised thousands of dollars for three of his favourite organizations. (Neil Burns)

Personal Participation

When my children were young, our annual visit to Cookshire Fair was a highlight of our summer. Although my own attendance at the Fair has been sporadic in recent years, I have continued to support the event by offering special prizes for the best display of farming photos by children, youth and adults.

For the past two years, I have rented a booth in the Main Building to sell my books and photography. I have also had the honour of presenting the 4-H Club's Mac Fraser Award trophy that is awarded annually in recognition of my brother's exceptional contribution to the Fair.

The Seed Fair

The summer/fall fair was not the only agricultural fair held in Cookshire. There was also a Seed Fair, usually held in January or February. This Compton County show was the only one of its kind in Quebec. Other fair boards held county seed exhibitions together with their summer fairs, but Compton was the only county to hold a separate event. Like the summer fair, the Seed Fair has gone through at least one reincarnation since its inception in the early 1900s. The exact date of the very first one is unknown, but a notice in the *Sherbrooke Daily Record* of January 6, 1917, referred to it as "The Annual Seed Fair."

Exhibit of baking beans at Compton County Seed Fair, ca. 1970 (photo by author)

After an absence of several decades, the Seed Fair made a reappearance in 1951. An article in the *Sherbrooke Daily Record* announced the event as a "Seed and Forage Crop Fair" sponsored by the Farm Forum and the Compton County Agricultural Society. A *Record* article on the Seed Fair's 30th anniversary describes the origins and purpose of the annual event:

Cookshire Fair

> Organizer Don MacMillan of Cookshire said the Fair is partly competition and partly education. "The Fair was founded by the late Tom Kirby in 1951," he said, "to improve cereal and forage crops in use in the region." And the gathering gives farmers a chance to learn about developments in the seed business. "We have a chance to advertise new products coming on the market, and discuss with the farmers which [of them] might be best suited to their particular operation." (*The Record*, Oct. 28, 1981)

My dad enthusiastically embraced the Seed Fair and came away with even more prizes than at the summer fair, as evidenced by *The Record's* publishing of the prize winners lists. Most noteworthy was the consistency of his winning first prize on turnips. Even at age 80, he was still the undisputed Turnip King of Compton

Seed, crop fair enjoyed

COOKSHIRE — The 22nd Annual Seed and Crop Fair was held in the Town Hall, Cookshire, under the auspices of the Compton County Agricultural Society in the Agronome's building, on Monday, March 12, 1973.

There was not as large an attendance as in previous years, only about 60 people attended; however, they were quite interested in the exhibits. The oats were not as good as usual, but the others were up to par. There were 12 exhibitors as compared to 17 the previous year, and 78 exhibits as compared to 84 the previous year.

The 1st vice-president, Mr. Malcolm Fraser, presided, and welcomed all. He thanked the directors, the secretary and agronome for their valuable assistance, and also those who had contributed prizes and prize money. He especially mentioned Mr. Walter Hodgman who had exhibited ever since the inception of the society, also Mr. Donald Fraser and Mr. R.G. Hodge. He mentioned the late Tom Kirby, who had contributed so much to the success of the society.

Mr. Fraser stated that it was unfortunate that the president, Mr. Fred Burns, was unable to be present, due to other demands on his time, but that he had been busy looking after the interests of the society, and that, contrary to rumors, there would definitely be a fair on the fair grounds in Cookshire this year, Aug 3-5. He urged all to participate in the various departments.

The local agronome was then asked for a few words, and stated how pleased he was to see so many young men taking hold of the various responsibilities of the seed fair, it augured well for the future, for without their help and support it would be non-existent. He also said that the judge, Mr. Jean Genest, of the Lennoxville Experimental Farm, had stated the weather conditions for the past year had not been very favorable for the crops.

Mr. Macmillan explained about zoning for the farmers and about the competitions which the government were sponsoring, and advised those wishing to compete, to get in touch with him at the agronome's office in Cookshire, for forms to be filled out, as soon as possible.

The prizes were then distributed by Mr. Fraser and Mr. Macmillan. Following is the list of special prizes awarded. Best display in classes 1 and 2 (oats) Walter Hodgman, $5.00, given by the Sherbrooke Co-op. Best exhibit in hay, 1st, Malcolm Fraser, given by D. Chapdelaine Inc., 2nd R.G. Hodge $4.00 in merchandise, given by J.A. Lowry. Best exhibit in potatoes, 1st Gordon McElrea, $3.00 merchandise given by C. Grondin, 2nd Wm French, $2.00 merchandise given by C. Grondin.

Highest aggregate in points won in regular classes, 1st, Ian Kirby, $3.00 in gas, given by Lynn's Texaco, Sawyerville; 2nd Donald Fraser, 25 lb. bag of flour, given by H.E Locke.

Judging competition. 1st highest aggregate, Judy Halsall, gift given by General Plastics. 2nd highest aggregate, Ross Kirby $5.00 in merchandise given by Sherbrooke Co-op.

Report on 1973 Seed Fair documents Fraser family involvement (*Sherbrooke Record*, March 19, 1973)

County. The 1978 Seed Fair was a family affair, as Malcolm took first prize on his oats and mixed hay entries.

- Feed turnips: 1st Donald Fraser; Table turnips: 2nd Donald Fraser (*Sherbrooke Daily Record*, Mar. 3, 1952)
- Feed turnips: 1st Donald Fraser; Table turnips: 1st Donald Fraser (*Sherbrooke Daily Record*, Mar. 22, 1962)
- Feed turnips: 1st Donald Fraser; Table turnips: 1st Donald Fraser (*Sherbrooke Record*, Nov. 4, 1978)

Whether it was the summer Cookshire Fair or the winter Seed Fair, there was one thing that could always be counted on – the participation of the Fraser family. As organizers and exhibitors, the people of Pine Hill Farm left their mark on these important agricultural events before passing the torch to a new generation of farmers.

Chapter 10
The Eaton River: From Salmon to Sawmills

Log drive on the Eaton River, 1894 (courtesy of Charles W. K. Fraser)

The Eaton River brings to mind the lyrics of the 1920s-era song "Ol' Man River":

> That ol' man river
> He don't say nothing
> But he must know something
> Cause he just keeps rolling
> He keeps rolling along
> Rollin' along
>
> He don't plant tators
> He don't plant cotton
> Them that plants 'em is soon forgotten
> But ol' man river
> He keeps rolling along

Since time immemorial, the Eaton River has been a feature of the land we call Pine Hill Farm. This willow-lined, winding waterway has been both a symbol of stability and a crucible of change. In this chapter we will explore different aspects of this dichotomy.

Transportation

Display on history of transportation in Haut-Saint-François region (Library and Archives Canada)

As mentioned earlier, until the late 1790s the only transportation routes were by water. In Eaton Township, the Eaton River served as the highway, for the Abenaki First Nations in their birchbark canoes and later for the settlers in flatboats. Both were forced to portage around falls and rapids. Gradually, roads were built, then bridges to cross the Eaton. John Cook, a fellow Associate of Orsamus Bailey, built the first one in 1830 – a wooden covered structure that still stands today even though the Eaton River, having had a new channel dug in about 1972, no longer flows under it.

Fishing

Before dams were built on the rivers by white settlers, the waters teemed with fish, including Atlantic salmon that fought their way upstream in the fall to spawn. The Abenaki camped on the banks of the rivers, including the Eaton, where they speared salmon. In an article in *Le Devoir*, journalist, author and Cookshire native

John Cook Covered Bridge over Eaton River, ca. 1980 (photo by author)

Jean-François Nadeau laments about how First Nations peoples lost their traditional fishing grounds:

> In Cookshire, my hometown, I grew up not far from the Eaton River. Some mornings, this Eastern Township river's water was green. On other days, it was red or a sort of blue-mauve. Sometimes it was even yellow or orange. The colour depended on that day's production of the Woollen Mills factory . . . During the time of the Abenakis, the river was called by a long name that I can't recall, but which meant "salmon river" . . . Until around 1875, one could fish for salmon in the Eaton River, as was the case for several Eastern Townships rivers. The first colonists, like the First Nations peoples, fed off them. One of the people most responsible for their disappearance was John Henry Pope, a very important figure in Cookshire and an influential member of Sir John A Macdonald's Conservative cabinet. By building water-powered sawmills to exploit the forest resources and increase his own wealth, Pope did not hesitate to impede the salmon's migration. (Jean-François Nadeau, "Les poissons" in *Le Devoir*, May 7, 2018; translated from French by author)

A similar reference to the Abenaki fishing grounds along the Eaton River occurs in Philippe Charland's 2005 McGill University thesis:

> The Eaton River ("Quamlawlaquake") . . . there were Abenakis living in the area, since colonization hadn't really started and [colonist] Coffin hired them to help him and hence effectively participate in their own dispossession of the land. As colonization progressed, the presence of Abenakis in the region obviously became more rare. Until the 1840s,

First Nations fisherman spearing salmon (bethelhistorical.org)

small groups of Abenakis from the village of St-Francis travelled up the rivers and installed seasonal camps in the area, including Cookshire during the 1830s. (Philippe Charland, "Définition et reconstitution de l'espace territorial du nord-est amériquain," translated from French by author)

In spite of the increased building of dams and sawmills, salmon did briefly return to the Eaton River in the late 1860s, as referenced in a Fisheries Department report:

> Mr. Welles reports salmon on the increase, and of larger growth than usual. They have returned to and spawned in the Eaton River, once famous for them, but where they had been of late years utterly exterminated, none having been seen there for thirty years. The fish-way erected on the mill dam at the mouth of the river doubtless admitted of their ascent. (Fisheries Department of Canada Annual Report, 1869)

Whale Bone Is Discovered Near Cookshire

A huge bone found by Victor Pare of Cookshire had this district in the geological dithers today.

But Canon Leon Marcotte, curator at Sherbrooke Seminary who was shown a picture of the bone, said it is the lower jam of some ancient marine animal, likely a whale.

Pare found the bone, however, in the Eaton river, a small stream not more than three feet deep.

Canon Marcotte said that ages and ages ago the "Champlain Sea" covered this part of the earth known as the Eastern Townships of Quebec. When the waters gradually subsided the giants of the sea remained.

The bone is 14 feet, two inches long, 14 inches wide and 24 inches in circumference. It weighs more than 200 pounds.

Article on whale bone discovery in Cookshire (*Sherbrooke Daily Record*, Apr. 20, 1951)

The Eaton River

A discovery in 1951 caused some to speculate that the Eaton River once contained even bigger "fish." The jaw of a bowhead whale was found in the river. Initially it was thought it might be a remnant from the prehistoric Champlain Sea. However, this theory was debunked by Canadian zoologist C. R. Harington:

> The Cookshire Quebec specimen. . . yielded a radiocarbon date of 750 +/- 60 BP (Beta 70094), so was definitely not of the Champlain Sea age, but was more likely transported inland by people (*homo sapiens*) . . . (C.R. Harington, "Annotated Bibliography of Quaternary Vertebrates of Northern North America with Radiocarbon Dates")

Lumbering

When its water level crested in spring, the Eaton River served the logging industry as the conduit from the upriver logging camps to the downriver sawmills. Lumberjacks who had worked in the woods all winter cutting wood then became log drivers in the spring, guiding the log booms down the rushing current. At the mill, the logs were hauled out of the river and stacked in the mill's huge wood yards. The inventoried logs would keep the mill in operation for many months. The local newspaper kept everyone updated on the status of the Cookshire mill's operation:

> The Cookshire Mill Company is repairing the mill preparatory to starting at work as soon as the logs come down the river. (*Compton County Chronicle*, Apr. 6, 1892)

Log driving on North River, 1800s (Eastern Townships Resource Centre)

Old logging chain buried in riverbank (photo by author)

Log drivers snow sculpture, Winterlude festival, Ottawa (photo by author)

The Eaton River

An 1894 detailed plan of the Eaton River in Cookshire indicates various elements related to the logging operations, including the locations of "cribs" and "booms" along the river, as well as the high-water levels. The plan also shows details of the mill and dam locations and identifies the nearby property owners, including C. I. Frasier (my grandfather and owner of Pine Hill Farm at that time).

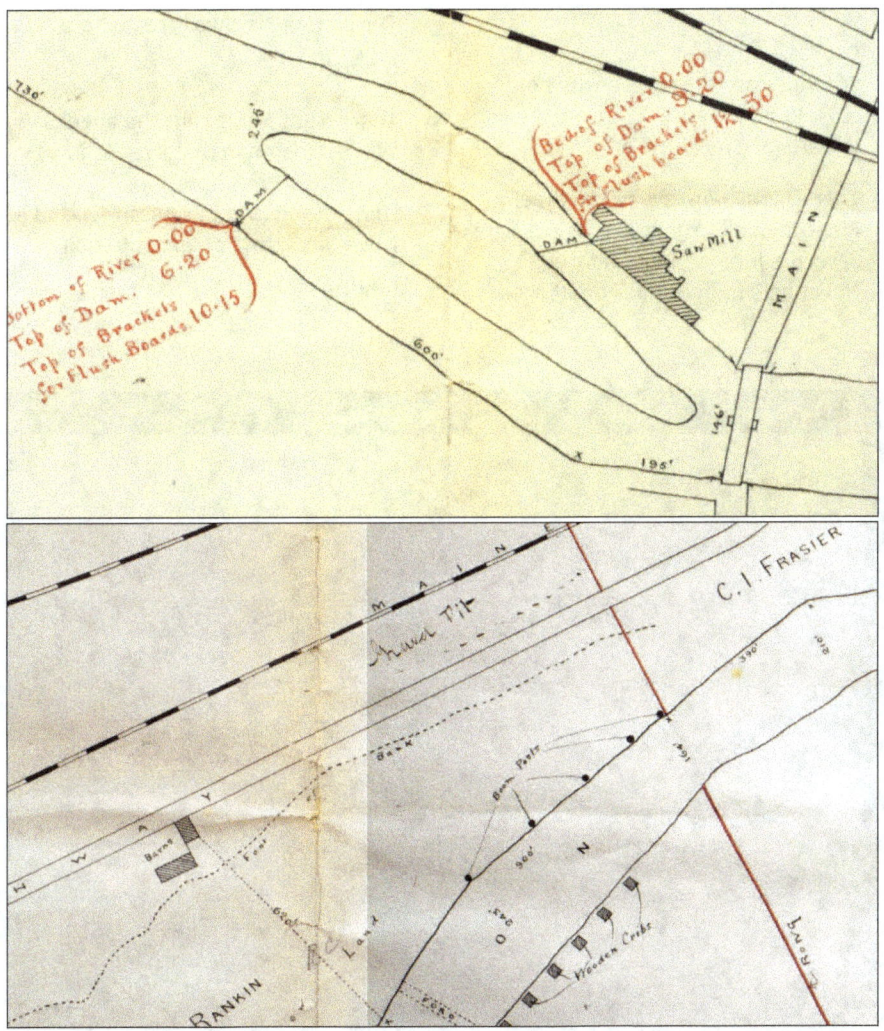

Eaton River Plan, 1894. Top: sawmill details ; above: Charles I. Frasier riverbank details (Eastern Townships Resource Centre)

Even though working in a sawmill was not an easy job, it appears that the Cookshire Mill Company's employees enjoyed good comradery, as indicated by a sampling of the many verses of The Cookshire Mill Song:

COOKSHIRE MILL SONG (composed by William Frazier, ca. 1890)

There's William Bailey is foreman still,
First to the office and then to the mill;
Unloads logs when they get behind,
And has an eye to business the rest of the time.

Chorus:
For those are the rules of the bold lumbermen;
We are jolly mill boys all.

There's Pinkham, always on time,
Rings the bell to give Barlow the sign;
Saws the lumber neat and free,
Never gets tight or goes on a spree.

(Chorus)

There's Le Page, who rolls the logs,
Handles the taps and drives the dogs;
Turns them over so quick and smart,
The carriage is always ready to start.

(Chorus)

There's Pat Burns runs the auger saw,
Wildest Irishman that ever used a paw;
Understands the business; sticks to it,
Never gets tired or wants to quit.

(Chorus)

Wood yard at Standard Chemical, Iron and Lumber Co., Cookshire, 1894 (Courtesy of Charles W. K. Fraser)

COOKSHIRE MILL SONG.

There's Ives and Pope, proprietors of Cookshire mill,
They own a gold mine, pockets well filled;
Ives is first to Ottawa, then back to the mill;
Says, "My boys, you shan't stand still."

CHORUS.
For those are the rules of the bold lumbermen;
We are jolly mill boys all.

There's William Bailey is foreman still,
First to the office and then to the mill;
Unload logs when they get behind,
And has an eye to business the rest of the time.

CHORUS.

There's Baker, Secretary for the mill,
You'll find him in the office with a good will.
Foots up the bills, passes them in;
That is the way to get the tin.

CHORUS.

At six in the morning, Barlow is the first to come,
To oil the engine so she'll run;
At half past six when the whistle blows,
To warn the men above theres no lack of steam below.

CHORUS.

There's Pinkham, always on time,
Rings the bell to give Barlow the sign;
Saws the lumber neat and true,
Never gets tight or goes on a spree.

CHORUS.

There's Le Page, who rolls the logs,
Handles the taps, and drives the dogs;
Turns them over so quick and smart,
The carriage is always ready to start.

CHORUS.

There's Pat Burns runs the auger saw,
Wildest Irishman that ever used a paw;
Understands the business; sticks to it,
Never gets tired or wants to quit.

CHORUS.

There's Geo. French, then comes in,
Trims all the lumber thick or thin,
And cuts it off any length you please,
Seems to do it with perfect ease.

CHORUS.

There's William Wilford always on hand,
Marks the lumber neat and grand.
Friendly, willing, full of fun;
Gives Rousseau lumber on the run.

CHORUS.

There's Jestin Veaue, runs the slab saw —
Is a good man to work — has no jaw.
When blocked up — frightened to death,
Then he goes for it right and left.

CHORUS.

There's Henry Laplant is a clever man —
Does as much work as any mill hand;
Butts the lumber, and saws it low;
Saws clapboards — keeps barber shop too.

CHORUS.

There's Tommy Cooper — I nearly left out,
A fine young fellow, so short and stout;
Saps the lumber so smooth and true,
Its fun to see him put it through.

CHORUS.

There's Willis Barlow — runs the drag saw —
Fine a lad as ever went to war.
Does the work neat and trim —
Is quite handy at any thing.

CHORUS.

Then there comes a steer log wheel,
Sit down on the rope; up with your heels;
But if the chain should break and go,
Clide French on the top shouts Ouillet out below.

CHORUS.

There's Willard, of course you all know
Is a great mill man, Ruf. Pope says so;
Gums the saws, files them too,
Makes them cut for the whole mill crew.

CHORUS.

There's George Noble, always around
To cull the lumber to see its sound;
Has the cars loaded in splendid shape;
A jolly good fellow — always wide awake.

CHORUS.

There's Horace Sawyer, the ex-sub Boss,
Resigned in a very good cause;
Up North River then did steer,
To scale the lumber, and see the deer.

CHORUS.

There's Fred Hurd — is under him,
Works so hard is getting thin.
His hard work, I understand,
Is playing poker, and holding a full hand.

CHORUS.

The boys say our pay is small,
When dollar a day will pay us all;
If Ives and Pope don't give us more pay,
We'll make a strike and go away.

CHORUS.

Fifteenth of the month when it does come,
Into the office William Bailey will run —
Cheer up! cheer up! without delay;
Fear not, my boy's for its pay-day.

CHORUS.

Mr. Bebo you must now be aware,
And of your lame horse take good care;
Be very careful whilst turning around,
And wide awake on the dumping ground.

CHORUS.

There's Charlie, the mill fireman, is German descent,
Came to Cookshire, house to rent.
If he would use dry wood, hide the green,
The boilers would be hot and plenty of steam;

CHORUS.

When the night watch comes to relieve the mill crew,
Cleans the mill all out anew,
Runs the engine, fires too,
Trims the lamps, and that will do.

CHORUS.

There's William Frazier who composed the mill song,
With Mr. Willard to hold him along;
If you are dissatisfied or uneasy still,
Craves your pardon with a good will.

CHORUS.

Cookshire Mill Song, ca. 1890 (Fraser family archives)

Farming

View of Eaton River and railways from farmhouse, ca. 1960 (photo by author)

Because the Eaton River flowed directly through our farm, separating the western high land from the eastern meadowlands, it played a very important role in the life of Pine Hill Farm. In fact, as a kid growing up, I thought we **owned** the river. After all, we crossed it at will, we sold gravel from its riverbed, and earlier generations cut and sold its ice in winter.

Cutting ice blocks (Eastern Townships Resource Centre)

Statements of revenue for river gravel sales, 1919 (above) and 1960 (right) (Fraser family archives)

The first thing my dad did every morning after coming downstairs was to tap the barometer shelf twice to see what the day's weather was going to be. Then he looked out the window at the Eaton River to see what the night's weather had been. The results of both of these actions had a significant impact on the day's farming activities. The impact of the first is obvious but the second is less so. In fact, knowing the river level was very important. It determined whether or not we could cross it at the normal spot directly below the farm, or if we would have to make an almost two-mile (3 km) detour through Cookshire (or, as we called it, "go around by town").

Spring flooding of the meadowlands was an ever-present threat. My earliest flood memory is from the late 1940s or early 1950s when I was knee-high to a grasshopper. I remember being recruited along with my siblings to "pick up sticks"

Vintage Pine Hill Farm ice tongs (photo by author)

Dad checking barometer for weather forecast (sketch by Elizabeth Fraser, 1992)

Oops! There goes half a load of hay down the river! (sketch by James Harvey)

from the meadowland fields that had been deposited by the sawmills upstream. My older sister, June, remembers that flood well: "We spent days picking up sticks and stones and loading them onto a 'stone boat.' I even found 37 cents in coins among the rubble – so for me it was a very profitable exercise!" Through the years, several other floods occurred that earned mention in the local newspapers:

> The C.P.R. are rebuilding the stone pier under the west end of railroad bridge across the Eaton river at Cookshire, which was washed out by the floods of last June. (*Sherbrooke Examiner*, Nov. 1, 1901)

> EATON RIVER AT HIGH WATER MARK: The continuous rains have brought the Eaton River up to high water mark. It has not been so high since the floods of 1901. The flats [meadowlands] are flooded, the basin road is under water, the water is flowing freely over the bridge and a number of houses are surrounded by water. (*Sherbrooke Daily Record*, Apr. 23, 1912)

> DAMAGE FROM FLOOD SEVERE IN COOKSHIRE: . . . the eastern portion of the town is completely inundated. Several farmers and townspeople have been forced to leave their homes. Roads leading to Bury, East Angus are impassable, in some places the water covering them to a depth or four to five feet . . . All the lowlands in this district are flooded

and some of the fields in the vicinity are covered with immense cakes of ice. Last night the water was as high as the time of the freshets last fall which caused considerable damage. (*Sherbrooke Daily Record*, Feb. 13, 1925)

16 FAMILIES ARE EVACUATED: Quebec police evacuated 16 families residing in a trailer park located beside the Eaton River here yesterday as flood waters slowly creep higher and higher . . . The flooding was caused by last weekend's high temperatures and precipitation forcing the river well above its normal level. (*Sherbrooke Record*, Mar. 23, 1976)

Family records show that, on multiple occasions, the Cookshire Mill Company paid compensation to my ancestors for "the damage done [to your] meadow by the logs and water which flooded same."

Compensation for flood damage, 1897 (top) and 1914 (above) (Fraser family archives)

Recreation

A surprising fact is we rarely went swimming in the river. My brother John (Jack), writing in a 1993 issue of the Fraser Family Link, makes mention of this:

> Mom's diary entry for July 3, 1949 notes "Very hot and close [humid]. John and June went to Church. Daddy, Marina, Malcolm and Winston went swimming down at the river." Now we know why some of the 12 excelled in swimming and others did not! (John "Jack" Fraser)

David Fraser in Eaton River swimming hole, ca. 1975 (courtesy of David Fraser)

Being only five years old at the time, I have no recollection of that rare occurrence. In any case, most of my siblings and I never learned to swim. However, our neighbours and other kids from the town made frequent use of the river to cool off on hot summer days. Even though the river was normally quite shallow in summer, there were some deeper parts that were amenable to swimming. Two persons share their memories:

> I remember being in the swimming hole in the Eaton River and watching your dad and some of the young folks crossing the river with the horses and hay wagon to go get hay on the other side. I don't remember ever seeing any of the Fraser kids go swimming there. (Dorothy Shelton Dionne)

The following recollection describes an Eaton River swimming adventure that had very unexpected consequences:

> It was the last day of school in 1951 and they let us out early. So my friends Donnie King, Ron Lafontaine, Bobby Gill, Mike Gage and myself decided to go for a swim in the Eaton River just below Pine Hill Farm. Usually we went to North River but this was closer. I recall that there was fairly swift moving water but to one side was a deeper lagoon with still water that was warmer. We had a great swim.
>
> A few days later I took ill with flu-like symptoms. As Dr. Bennett was

away, Dr. Lepine was called. He diagnosed a pain in the belly and told my mother I'd be all right in a few days. When I continued getting worse, I was taken to Dr. Lowry's clinic in Sawyerville. He took blood and stool samples and sent them by bus to Sherbrooke. That night all hell broke loose when the doctor returned with Suzanne Larochelle, the county nurse. The diagnosis was typhoid fever. Our house was immediately quarantined – I was not let out of my room and my mother was not let out of the house. No one was allowed in or out – not even my dad, who was mayor at the time. And the news had to be contained for fear of causing a public panic. The nurse spent about 12 hours a day with us. The medication I was given lasted about ten days, tasted horrible, and left me with a bad taste in my mouth as well as bad breath. After about three days, all my body hair (arms, legs, head, private areas) fell out so that I was truly as bald as a baby. The illness lasted about two weeks but then I had to have blood tests every two weeks till late in the fall.

Meanwhile, the health clinic was desperately trying to find the source. Initially they gave Richie Mackay a hard time because he was our milkman. Eventually they deemed that Fraser's swimming hole was the culprit. The water had been polluted due to Sawyerville dumping their garbage into the river. Authorities closed that dump as well as the one in Cookshire where the rest area and picnic grounds are today. They also sent in heavy equipment and changed the channel in the river so that it would move more swiftly – on the pretext that it would help prevent ice jams in the spring.

It was only years later, when I was working with Mrs. Thompson to bring students from the Lower North Shore, that I realized how fortunate I had been. Many typhoid patients from that region had died of the disease. (Rodger Heatherington)

In the winter, my grandfather's family went skating and played hockey on the frozen waters of the Eaton, according to a photograph from the early 1900s.

Goodbye Meadowlands

In 2013, the Pine Hill Farm meadowland – 40 acres (16 ha) of flat, fertile, stone-free land – was sold to neighbouring farmer Graham Hodge, whose ancestors settled in nearby Learned Plain in the early 1800s. In fact, the Hodge family had a connection to Orsamus Bailey, the original settler of Pine Hill Farm:

David Hodge was born in Burney, N. H., and married Catherine Sunbury, of Massachusetts. They moved into Eaton in 1800. He settled on lots six and seven in the seventh range, where he cleared one of the finest farms in town, and which is now occupied by his grandsons, Alonzo and Alton. When first coming to Eaton he worked for Orsamus Bailey, and felled the first tree on what is known as the Ward Bailey meadow, Cookshire. (L. S. Channell, *History of Compton County*, 1896)

Skating and hockey on Eaton River, ca. 1910 (Fraser family archives)

David Fraser relaxing on Eaton River "beach," ca. 1975 (courtesy of David Fraser)

Sale of Pine Hill Farm meadowland from Malcolm Fraser to Graham Hodge, 2013 (Fraser family archives)

Archaeological dig on west bank of the Eaton River, Oct. 2019 (photo by author)

Teenage sisters Marina and June Fraser at Eaton River, ca. 1950 (Fraser family archives)

Through the years, the Eaton River has played an important role for First Nations peoples and for the farmers of Pine Hill Farm. Although its use has changed drastically, it is still an attractive feature of the local landscape as it "keeps rolling along."

Chapter 11
The Town of Cookshire: Proximity and Partnership

Postcard of bird's-eye view of Cookshire, ca. 1900 (author's collection)

Because of its proximity, Pine Hill Farm has always had a unique and close relationship with the town of Cookshire. For example, it wasn't clear whether our farm was located in the country or in town. In one sense, with the large open fields, the dense forest and the lack of any very close neighbours, we definitely felt like we were in the country. On the other hand, we were within walking distance of school, churches and stores, so we felt like we were part of the town. In fact, according to the original and current official cadastral maps, the entire Pine Hill Farm property – including the woods and the sugar bush – was/is located within the town boundaries. Since we always walked to and from school, our teachers considered us "town kids." But when our parents took us out of class to help with farm work, they realized we were really "country kids"! Personally, I enjoyed living this duality – it was the best of both worlds.

A Special Place

I always took pride in being a citizen of Cookshire – proud of its roots, proud of its charm and proud of its people. The following historical perspectives encapsulate some of those sentiments:

In summer, the place has a delightfully cool and refreshing appearance, as from the rising grounds may be seen the white farmhouses and their clusters of outbuildings, in pleasing contrast with the beautiful green of the trees, pastures and fields; and occasionally a glittering spire pointing heavenward, while in some directions a background is formed to the scene by prominent mountains. Of these, the Stoke Mountains are on the northwest; the Megantic [Mountains] on the east; the Hereford hills on the south, while still farther in the distance are the pale blue outlines of prominent peaks beyond the Provincial line. (L. S. Channell, *History of Compton County*, 1896)

Cookshire is a delightful residential village, and its well-kept properties and beautiful memorial park merit the admiration so often expressed by tourists. The village boasts of unlimited power, plenty of pure drinking water, two hotels, two banks, two fine schools, three churches and all the conveniences of a city combined with the charm of country life . . . Cookshire is built on the western slope of the valley of the Eaton River, and commands a fine view of one of the most picturesque sections of the Province of Quebec. One of the most popular highways leading from the New England States into the province and on to Quebec City passes through the village and affords the tourists glimpses of water and landscape views of rare charm and beauty. (*Sherbrooke Daily Record*, Feb. 25, 1933)

History

Cookshire has a rich and interesting history, from prehistoric times right up to the present. The town's website includes the following facts in its historical summary:

- The Abenakis were the first people to set camp along the Eaton River.
- Around 1793, Josiah Sawyer, an American, was one of the first colonists to settle with his family near the Eaton River. He gave his name to the town of Sawyerville.
- The American John Cook settled in the area around the same time. Cookshire was named in his honour. The town was officially founded in 1892. The first general store was built in 1830, on the corner of the streets known today as Craig and Principale.
- In the second half of the 19th century, the Cookshire-Eaton area gained nation-wide renown in agriculture, railways, forestry, and the military. The administrative, judiciary and political services for Compton County were all located on its territory. (cookshire-eaton.qc.ca)

Currently the town of Cookshire is part of the "urban agglomeration" of Cookshire-Eaton that also includes the village of Sawyerville and the townships of Newport and Eaton. Its total population as of the Canada 2011 Census was 5,171.

Although today the population of Cookshire and area is more than 90% francophone, it was once majority anglophone, as explained in a 2011 Townshippers' Association paper:

> The historical Eastern Townships is one of the few places in Quebec where the first European settlers were not French speakers. When the region was opened for settlement in 1792, the first wave of homesteaders came from the American colonies, followed by a second wave from the British Isles. In 1861, it was home to a numerically strong English-speaking population, comprising 58% of the total population. (Joanne Pocock and Brenda Hartwell, "Profile of the English-speaking Community in the Eastern Townships," townshippers.qc.ca)

However, this changing demographic did not appear to have any significant impact on the people of Pine Hill Farm and their relationship with the community. Although he spoke very little French, my dad interacted comfortably with his francophone neighbours. Several of us siblings became bilingual, most notably Malcolm, who became postmaster and sat on the town council.

CAP. LVII.

An Act to incorporate the town of Cookshire.

[Assented to 24th June, 1892.]

Preamble. WHEREAS the provisions of the Municipal Code do not meet the requirements of the inhabitants of the village of Cookshire, and it has become necessary to make more ample provisions for the management and control of their municipal affairs; and whereas the said inhabitants are desirous of obtaining a special act of incorporation, and application has been duly made to that effect;

Therefore, Her Majesty, by and with the advice and consent of the Legislature of Quebec, enacts as follows:

Inhabitants of town incorporated.
Name.
Separated from county for municipal purposes.
General powers.

1. From and after the passing of this act, the inhabitants of the town of Cookshire, as hereinafter described and bounded, and their successors shall be and they are hereby declared to be a body corporate and politic, by the name of the "Corporation of the town of Cookshire," separate from the county of Compton, for all municipal purposes.

As such corporation, they and their successors shall have perpetual succession, and shall be capable of appearing in law, of suing and of being sued, of pleading and of being impleaded in all courts, actions, causes and plaints whatsoever; they shall have a common seal, which they may change or modify at their pleasure, and shall be capable of receiving by gratuitous title, of acquiring, holding and alienating, by any title, or in any manner whatsoever, any

Excerpt of Act to incorporate the town of Cookshire (Quebec Session Laws, 1892)

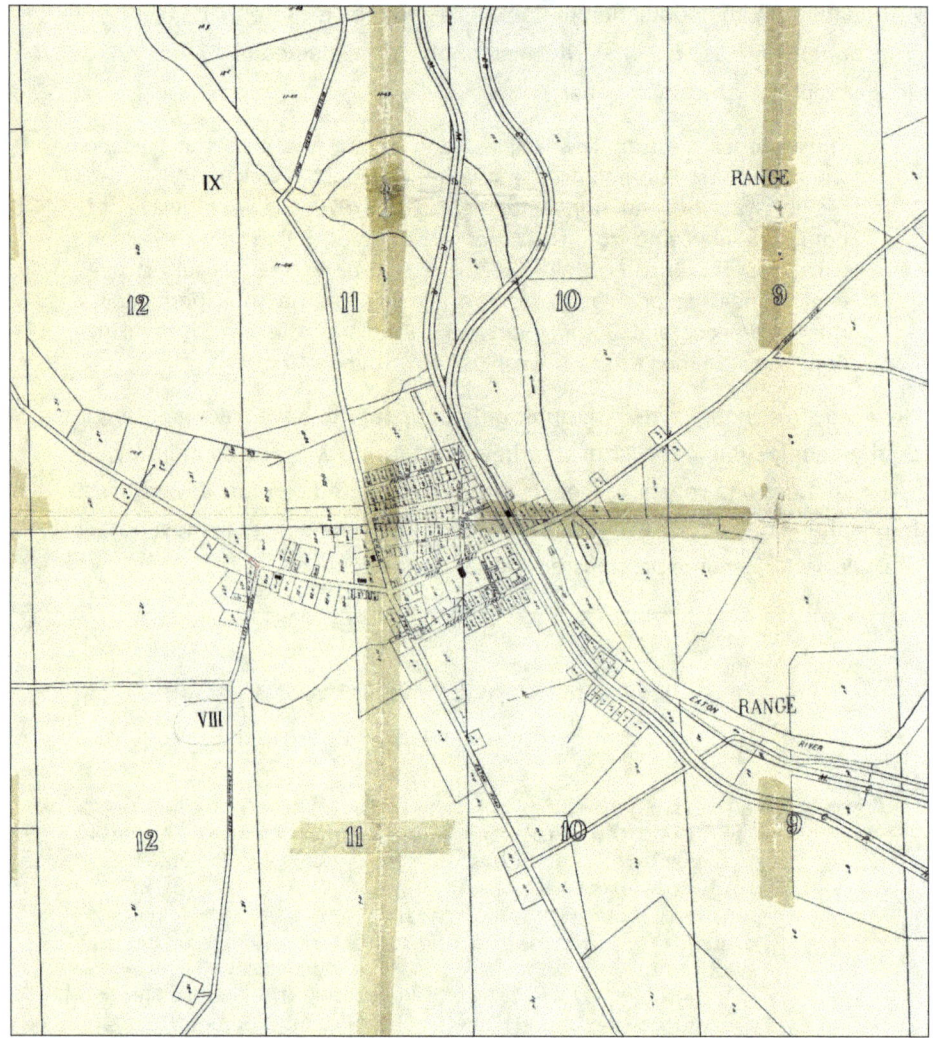

Plan of Cookshire, 1917 (histoiresherbrooke.ca)

An old document recently discovered amongst my family papers sheds light on the early life of Cookshire's founder:

> According to the records in the possession of descendants, the Late John Cook Sr. left his home in Connecticut at the age of 21 years during the fall of 1795 to make a home under the British Flag. He was accompanied by a friend 19 yrs. of age who in later years returned to the United States. They proceeded North with guns and packs walking most of the way to Northern Vermont. At the last Supply Station they replenished their packs with sea biscuit or hard-tack, ammunition, axes and a few small implements. They soon entered the virgin forest, where white man had never trod; somewhere near the present site of Canaan Vt., and made

their path spotting the trees with axes (so as to return by the same route) as far as the Eaton River not far from its source, followed it down to the present site of the present town of Cookshire. Just below the present town near the C.P.R. Station, he found a stretch of many acres covered with majestic pine and spruce, while the uplands were well watered with babbling springs and decided to camp on a rise not far from the present home of C. W. Cook. Here he cleared land, seeded and built a commodious dwelling, making a home to receive his wife the next Fall. He then prevailed upon twelve of his associates to join him, naming their little village Cooks-Shire which was changed after his death in 1819 to Cookshire. (author unknown, "Reminiscences of Early Cookshire")

Cook was also mentioned in the Attleborough Ledger. His page in the travelling salesman's account book, headed "Capt. Cook, John" contained the following entries:

- 1809 August 5: 1 bed stead 2.00
- Sept 18th to myself: 9 1/2 days work; 11 1/2 days work at one dollar per day 21.00; one day work 1.00
- November 1816: making coffin 1.50
- Sept 1829 Mrs. Cook: table 4.00; stand 2.00; 2 bed steads 4.00; rakes 1.50; 6 dining chairs 9.00; rocking chair back 3.50
- [total] 24.00

So, exactly when was Cookshire first called by that name? The preceding account by the unknown source seems to agree with this 1893 newspaper article excerpt: "The town received its name from John Cook. It was first called this by Colonel Taylor after Mr. Cook's death [in 1820]." (*Compton County Chronicle*, Dec. 20, 1893)

However, in the course of my research I came across something most interesting amongst Josiah Sawyer's land grant papers. A handwritten document, dated 1799

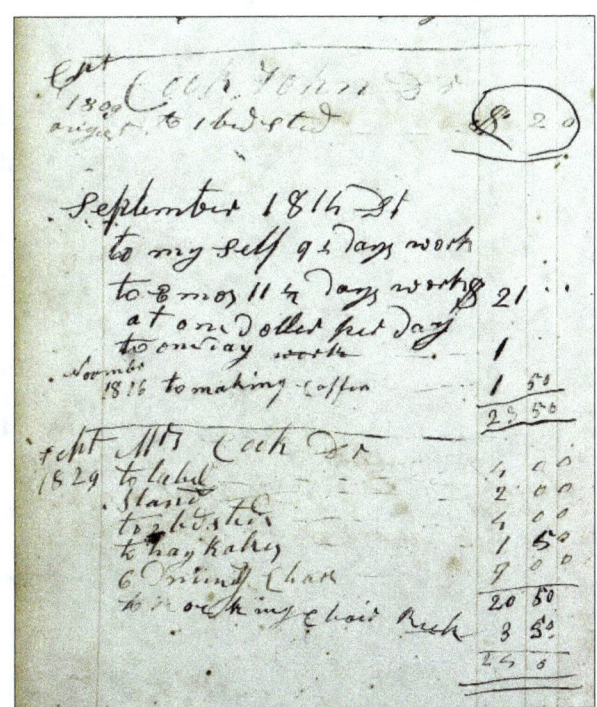

Capt. John Cook account in Attleborough Ledger, 1809-1829 (numerique.banq.qc.ca)

Turnip harvest with Cookshire in background, ca. 1957 (photo by author)

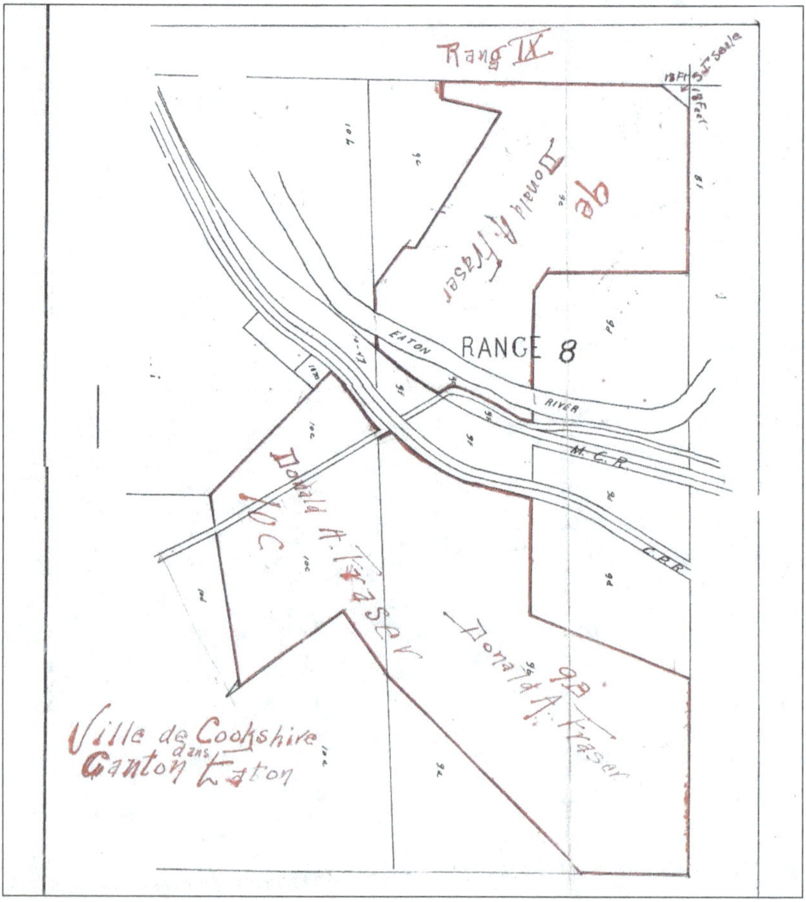

Pine Hill Farm indicated on Town of Cookshire plan, ca. 1950s (Fraser family archives)

> There's a settlement called Cookshire, where there's a school already established, that has thirty scholars, where children are taught to read, to write, and to cipher.

Josiah Sawyer's earliest mention of Cookshire, 1799 (Library and Archives Canada, digitally enhanced by Jim Fraser)

and signed by Sawyer, contained the following text: "In this Township on a branch of the River Saint Francis there's a settlement called Cookshire where there's a school already established, that has thirty scholars, where children are taught to read, to write and to cipher." It was quite fascinating to learn that our beloved town was called Cookshire almost 100 years before it was officially incorporated in 1892.

It is impossible to discuss the history of Cookshire without mentioning the name of her most prominent citizen, John Henry Pope. His primordial role in bringing the railway to Cookshire has already been covered in Chapter 7. Here we will describe Pope's lesser-known but equally important national unity role, as told by his son, Senator Rufus Pope in a 1927 Jubilee Celebration speech in Cookshire:

> Hon. John Henry Pope, as a young man on his farm, was driven into public life as a protest against an effort that was being made in favor of annexation [to the United States]. When Mr. Pope was approached re annexation to the U.S.A, the young man was busy shingling his house. His reply was "No, sir" and he threw down his hammer and said "You will not get one signature in this town," and he followed from house to house and drove the petitions away without a [single] signature. This was the commencement of Mr. Pope's public activities. (*Sherbrooke Daily Record*, July 6, 1927)

Merchants

For a small town, Cookshire seemed to have a lot of merchants. In fact, before my time, there were even more. A hand-drawn Cookshire map from the 1930s (courtesy of Almon Pope who acquired it from Colin Standish) lists no less than 75 places of business and other public spaces!

Most of our family's business was done with only a few merchants. Some others were patronized just occasionally and the rest had to survive without our family's business. Following are some I particularly remember from my formative years, the 1950s:

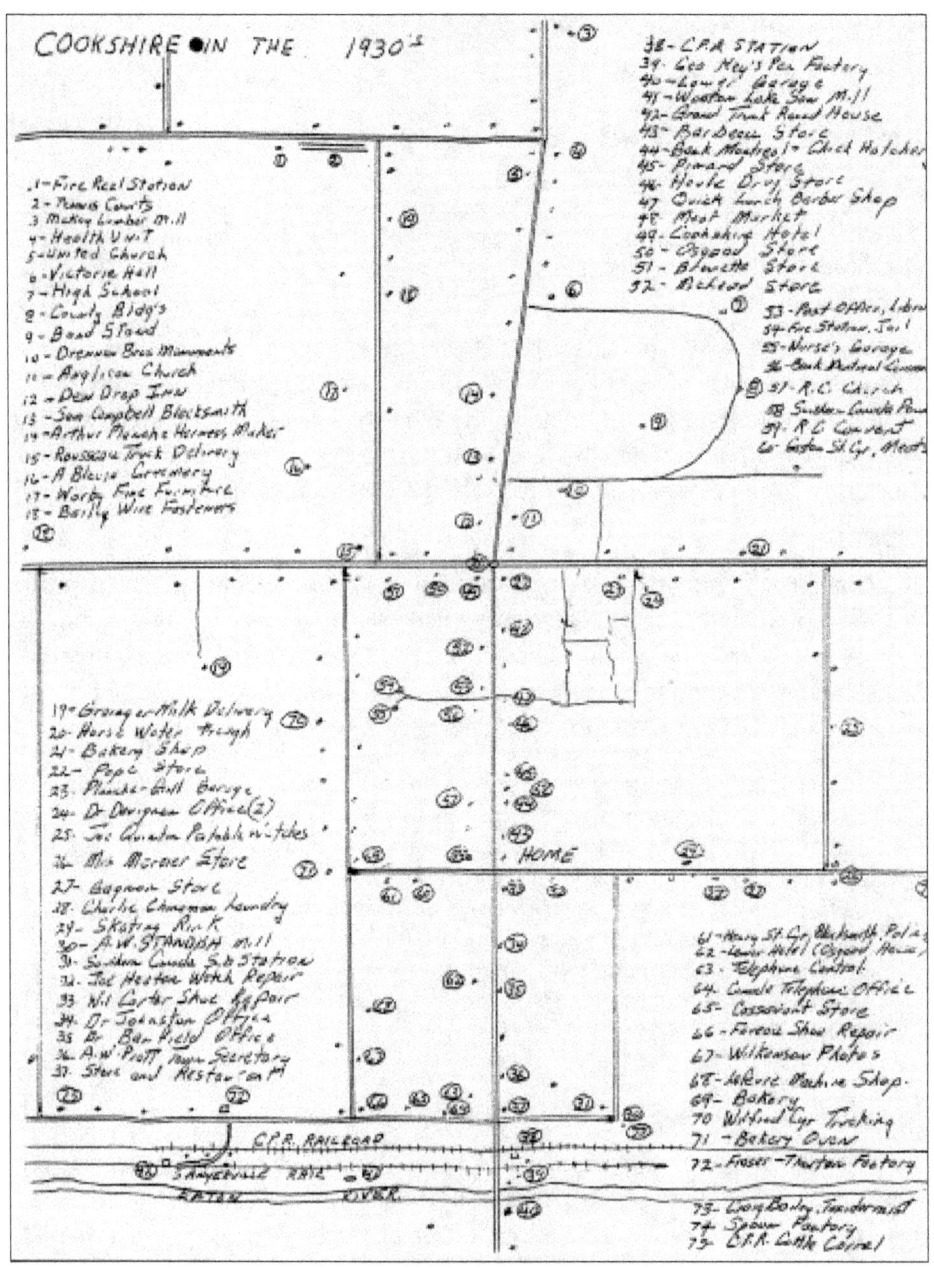

Hand-drawn map of Cookshire in the 1930s (courtesy of Almon Pope)

The Town of Cookshire

Cookshire Places of Business and Public Spaces
(as identified on the hand-drawn map opposite)

1- Fire Reel Station	39- Geo. Key's Pen Factory
2- Tennis Courts	40- Lower Garage
3- McKay Lumber Mill	41- Wooton Lake Saw Mill
4- Health Unit	42- Grand Trunk Round House
5- United Church	43- Barbeau Store
6- Victoria Hall	44- Bank Montreal & Chick Hatchery
7- High School	45- Pinard Store
8- County Bldgs.	46- Houle Drug Store
9- Band Stand	47- Quick Lunch Barber Shop
10- Drennan Bros. Monuments	48- Meat Market
11- Anglican Church	49- Cookshire Hotel
12- Dew Drop Inn	50- Osgood's Store
13- Sam Campbell Blacksmith	51- Brouette's Store
14- Arthur Planche Harness Maker	52- McLeod's Store
15- Rousseau Truck Delivery	53- Post Office, Library
16- A. Blouin Creamery	54- Fire Station, Jail
17- Worby Fine Furniture	55- Nurse's Garage
18- Bailey Wire Fasteners	56- Bank Montreal-Commerce
19- Grainger Milk Delivery	57- R.C. Church
20- Horse Water Trough	58- Southern Canada Power
21- Bakery Shop	59- R.C. Convent
22- Pope's Store	60- Gaston St. Cyr Meats
23- Planche-Gill Garage	61- Henry St. Cyr Blacksmith, Police
24- Dr. Davignon Office	62- Lower Hotel (Osgood House)
25- Joe Quintin Portable Watches	63- Telephone Central
26- Mrs. Mercier Store	64- Canada Telephone Office
27- Gagnon Store	65- Casavant's Store
28- Charlie Chinaman Laundry	66- Favreau Shoe Repair
29- Skating Rink	67- Wilkinson Photos
30- A. W. Standish Mill	68- Lefevre Shoe Repair
31- Southern Canada Substation	69- Bakery
32- Joe Heston Watch Repair	70- Wilfred Cyr Trucking
33- Wil Carter Shoe Repair	71- Bakery Oven
34- D.r Johnston Office	72- Frasier, Thornton Factory
35- Dr. Banfield office	73- Craig Bailey Taxidermist
36- A. W. Pratt Town Secretary	74- Spoon Factory
37- Store & Restaurant	75- CPR Cattle Corral
38- CPR Station	

The main merchant for us was S. J. Osgood & Sons, known simply as Osgood's to us. They provided everything from oranges to corn flakes to toilet paper. Many of my siblings shared the unique pleasure of phoning in the weekly order to chief cashier Henrietta Hodgman. A couple of hours later, Gerry Osgood would deliver the goods to the house. (I once worked at Osgood's store, though my employment lasted only one day. After spending most of the day in the cellar sorting beer bottles, I called it quits!)

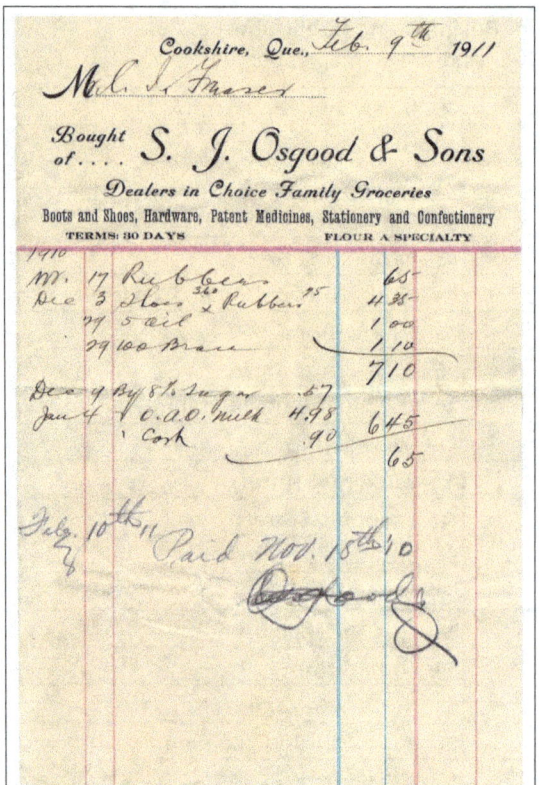

Charles Ira Fraser invoice from S. J. Osgood & Sons, 1911 (Fraser family archives)

A.H. Pope & Son was another merchant we used on a fairly regular basis. I can't recall what we bought there, but I think it was goods that came in bulk, because I remember the huge barrels in front of the counter. Allie Pope also sold customized panes of glass which he cut on a large board that covered the sugar barrel! He must have sold regular groceries too, because I recall his son Lionel delivering the order. We kids also sold Allie Pope the beer bottles and soft drink bottles we collected on the roadsides, earning five cents and two cents apiece respectively.

Hurd's Meat Market undisputedly had the best meat in town, even though we didn't often order the best cuts. Nonetheless, the bacon ends and stewing bones were very good. Fred Hurd and Don Macrae, neatly attired in their white aprons, were always friendly and accommodating.

Uncle Ken's Dew Drop Inn offered a treasure trove of candies, chocolates, ice cream, greeting cards, comic books and girlie magazines. Not to mention cigarettes ("coffin nails"), Coke ("big poison") and Pepsi ("little poison"). This was a store that never had a cash register – only a sculpted wooden cash drawer under the counter. The items purchased were tallied up in pencil on the front of a brown paper bag and, of course, we were always treated with "family pricing." Buying

Charles Ira Fraser invoice from H. H. Pope, 1898 (Fraser family archives)

something at the Dew Drop Inn, however, was always a long process because of Uncle's friendly and talkative nature.

Casavant's (also known as Goff's) contained a mixture of dry goods, hardware and clothing. All items were marked with a secret code indicating the cost price (i.e., how much the store paid for the item) that Dad was able to interpret, so he knew exactly what the markup was. I remember that the floor creaked a lot and that the store had a very unique scent. Mom and Dad might have bought clothing there prior to Mom establishing a special relationship with Au Bon Marché in Sherbrooke.

Not far from Casavant's was the shoemaker, Sylvio Lapierre. Although he repaired our shoes occasionally, his main specialty was horse harnesses. It was quite amazing how he was able to create a complete harness from scratch with all the buckles, rings, straps, etc.

Although Frasier, Thornton & Co. did not have a store per se, we kids would occasionally be sent to "The Factory" to purchase various patent medicines, including Muscalene, Panacea and Wild Strawberry Extract. I remember the place as being quite scary and full of pungent odours. During the latter years of my time in Cookshire, Madame Carrier operated a drugstore that I feared entering because of her ferocious little ankle-biter dog.

Wallace Silversmiths was not really a merchant either, but I think they did sell silverware sets to the local public. A similar situation existed for the Woollen Mills and the plastics factory that came later. Drennan Bros. was a long-established gravestone merchant, located beside the County Building and the school. It later became Kipling's. Mr. Canuel had a jewellery and watch repair shop on Craig Street just beyond Allie Pope's. I remember the large clock that hung on a post outside his shop.

The Green Lantern and the Royal Café were the only restaurants in town (apart from the Dew Drop Inn). I don't remember eating in either of them but I do recall the annual trips to the Green Lantern to buy ice cream to celebrate the end of haying (usually about two days before it was time to go back to school!). And we must not forget the local watering hole, the Osgood House Hotel.

Cookshire had an abundance of garages, none of which we frequented very often because we never had a car. There was neighbour Georges Loignon's Garage, Bruno Turcotte's Garage near the river, and Charlie Mathieu's Garage where we sometimes took our bikes to put air in the tires or to get them repaired.

Several merchants catered to the needs of area farmers: Donat Chapdelaine's Mill (to grind oats and other grains); Georges Beaulieu's Cooperative (or "Corporative" as Dad used to call it) for animal feed, fertilizer, fencing, etc.; Jos. St-Cyr's blacksmith shop; and Willie Foley's machine shop (for repairing farm equipment). And we must not forget merchants such as electrician Elmer Heatherington, seamstress Mademoiselle Migneault and "Regardless" Seale, the radio repair guy.

Pine Hill Farm always had a close two-way relationship with the merchants of Cookshire. Local stores were patronized for the purchase of food, clothing, household supplies, livestock feed and farm equipment. In exchange, some of the merchants bought various farm produce, including dairy products, maple products, vegetables and meats. In some cases, there was no money involved in the transaction – the value of goods bought exactly balanced the value of goods sold.

Special Events

Cookshire has always been a place where people gathered together to celebrate many kinds of events, and the Frasers were faithful supporters. Indeed, in some cases, our family played a key leadership role in their planning and execution.

Some of these celebrations, like the annual Cookshire Fair (covered in detail in Chapter 9) go back more than 100 years. Others, such as the Festival du Pain (Bread Festival), were very popular for several years before running their course. My brother Malcolm was deeply involved in the organization of both these events.

Besides these major annual events, there were numerous "one-time" celebrations. Following is a small sampling of some that were reported in the local press:

Mr. Crust greets Frasers at Cookshire's 1981 Bread Festival (Festival du Pain) (photo by author)

- Peace Day celebration, 1919
- Victoria Day celebration, 1924
- Jubilee celebration, 1927
- Cookshire Roman Catholic Church Centennial, 1968
- Cookshire High School Centennial, 1984
- Town of Cookshire Centennial, 1992
- Cookshire Anglican Church 150th Anniversary, 2017

Above: Ad for Victoria Day celebration (*Sherbrooke Daily Record*, May 21, 1924)

Right: Report of Cookshire Peace Day celebration (*Sherbrooke Daily Record*, July 21, 1919)

During the morning and early afternoon the Cookshire Concert Band, under the leadership of Mr. Joseph D. Blanchard, paraded through the principal streets of the town discoursing patriotic music and appropriate airs, which added greatly to the celebration of the day. About a thousand people assembled in town from the surrounding towns and villages, and an automobile parade, some of the cars being suitably decorated with the national colors and flags of the Allies, took place. The parade was led by Mayor F. R. Cromwell, accompanied by Senator Rufus H. Pope, Mrs. Cromwell and Mrs. Pope. On arriving at the band stand on the county grounds, the assemblage was addressed by Mr. Thomas Brooks Fletcher, of the Community Chautauqua, who was especially invited to return here for these demonstrations. Mr. Fletcher gave a most eloquent and inspiring address and received a great ovation, as did Senator Pope, who followed him as the next speaker and who spoke on "Duty" and "Imperialism." After this, the majority of the listeners attended the Chautauqua events in the afternoon and evening, and the day's celebration was brought to a close by a two hours dance in Victoria Hall, which was largely attended after the Chautauqua performance, at which the attraction was Tasca's Banda Rossa.

Celebration of Old Home Week in front of J. H. Pope residence, 1870 (author's collection)

Cookshire Centennial parade on Main Street, 1992 (photo by author)

Fraser brothers Winston (with wooden yoke and sap pails) and Malcolm (wearing top hat) with Fraser's maple sugaring float for Saint-Camille de Cookshire Roman Catholic Church Centennial celebration, 1968 (photo courtesy of Janice Fraser)

The first three of these events featured performances of the Cookshire Concert Band in which my dad played the slide trombone. For the later celebrations, my brother Malcolm was one of the leading organizers.

Malcolm and Cookshire School Centennial plaque, 1984 (photo by author)

Gone But Not Forgotten

Dew Drop Inn Cookshire postcard, ca. 1945 (courtesy of Chris Standish)

Many of the Cookshire buildings I knew so well have departed the town's landscape forever. Like the train station, where I used to go and be mesmerized watching the telegraph operator doing Morse code. Or the Dew Drop Inn, where I never got tired of listening to my uncle's stories and where I could buy an ice

Fred and Mary Noble's house, ca. 1965 (photo by author)

Osgood House Hotel (stampauctionnetwork.com)

Charlie Mathieu's Garage and Standish Bros., ca. 1950s (Malcolm Fraser collection)

A. H. Pope & Son's store, ca. 1950s (Malcolm Fraser collection)

Georges Loignon's Garage, Hurd's Meat Market (mostly hidden), and Dew Drop Inn, ca. 1950s (Malcolm Fraser collection)

Maplemount, Charles Clark Fraser's residence after its conversion to a "home for young folk," ca. 1970 (Fraser family archives)

cream cone for a nickel. Or Cousin Charlie's stately Maplemount home, whose extensive lawns I mowed with an old manual push lawnmower. Or Fred and Mary Noble's beautiful two-storey brick home, where I worked as charlady for five cents an hour. Or the gaudy and smelly Frasier, Thornton & Co. factory, where we'd be sent for cure-all medicines. Or even the Osgood House Hotel, where my dad's brother, Kenneth, delivered milk and cream every day and fell in love with the chambermaid. Yes, all these buildings are gone but will never be forgotten.

Thanks to the efforts of people like local businessman Gilles Denis, some of Cookshire's other heritage structures have escaped the fate of merciless demolition. Venerable Victoria Hall and historic St. Peter's Anglican Church rectory are just two such examples.

Victoria Hall and vintage car show, ca. 1984 (photo by author)

Maison de la Culture John-Henry-Pope, formerly St. Peter's Church Rectory, 2017 (photo by author)

Unfortunately, not every preservation effort is successful, as illustrated by my own personal experience:

Back in 1993, after the Cookshire railway station had been abandoned for several years and was scheduled to be demolished, I came up with an idea to save the station and give it a new life. I contacted CPR with my plan to purchase the station and move it to Quebec Lodge Camp on Lake Massawippi where it would serve as the camp office. CPR responded positively to my proposal and sent me a purchase contract whereby I could purchase the building for a cost of $1. Although the price was right, there were some problematic clauses in the proposed agreement. For example, I would be responsible for the total "clean-up" of the station site, which would cost approximately $5000. On top of that would be the cost of moving the building to its new site, estimated to be at least another $5000. Thus, my well-intentioned idea to save the station failed and soon afterwards, this historic Cookshire landmark was sadly demolished. However, I did first rescue a souvenir – a bamboo hoop for passing orders to a passing train's crew.

Above: Souvenir train conductor message passer

Right: Inside abandoned Cookshire railway station, 1993

(photos by author)

For more than 200 years, the town of Cookshire and Pine Hill Farm have had a mutually beneficial relationship. It has been a partnership facilitated by proximity and realized through support and participation.

Cookshire Academy classes, ca. 1910 (Malcolm Fraser collection)

Chapter 12
Memories, Miracles, Mysteries and Musings

The majestic white pines of Pine Hill Farm, ca. 1980 (photo by author)

In the preceding chapters, we have offered a salubrious smorgasbord of historical facts and figures as main course. Shortly we will bring on the dessert. Featured on our menu will be a scrumptious selection of the stuff that makes life exciting: family feuds, unsolved mysteries and amazing miracles. But first, I will briefly lend my pen (Oops – I mean my keyboard) to others who wish to share their own personal memories of Pine Hill Farm.

Visitor Viewpoints

It is interesting how visitors often see a place quite differently from those who live there. To them, a visit to Pine Hill Farm was nothing but fun, fun, fun, whereas for us it seemed to be interminable work, work, work! Of course we did have some fun times but they were largely overshadowed by the busyness of farm work. In a 1993 issue of the Fraser Family Link, my brother Warren put it all into perspective.

Visitors Muriel, Judy and Terry French holding Fraser geese, 1947 (courtesy of Muriel French Fitzsimmons)

> As a young teen growing up on Pine Hill Farm – although I never realized it then – Mom and Dad made me realize that farming isn't all bad. It involves much hard work and long hours with little remuneration, but at the end of each day, you are left with the knowledge that you have accomplished something worthwhile no matter how insignificant it may seem to others. (Warren Fraser)

My dad was never excited about having visitors – especially young kids – when we were trying to work. As a result, he would sometimes devise schemes to rid himself of unwanted "help." I recall one such incident in particular. One winter Saturday, Almon Pope, a good friend of my younger siblings, came to "help" us cut wood. My dad didn't necessarily consider extra "visitors" to be of much help. So, after a few minutes, he would expose one ear from under his cap, cup his ear with his hand, look heavenward and say in a very loud voice "OK, LIONEL; I'LL SEND HIM RIGHT HOME!" Then he would tell young Almon that he heard his dad calling him. So the boy would obediently leave, running all the way home. Of course, when he arrived at his house more than a mile away, he would discover that his dad wasn't calling him after all. About an hour later, Almon would be back, ready to "help" once more!

Several Pine Hill Farm visitors, including non-resident family and friends, share their memories of the place that they called "the farm" and that I still call "home."

> I remember your cellar under the house with all those turnips in boarded bins. I remember the spring water source just behind the lower barn and

the one along Railroad Street (I drank from it many times). I remember the wild roses that lined Fraser Road on both sides from the house and barn down to the intersection with Railroad Street. They smelled so wonderful. I remember those huge lovely white pines in front of the house, and how they would sway gently in the breeze. I remember how Malcolm would entertain us by squirting milk from the cow's teat into an anxiously awaiting cat's mouth when Gail and I would go into the barn at milking time. I fondly remember our Sunday ball hockey games on the road just above the barn where the road was a bit flatter, with Steve, Warren, David, Jimmy, their Bellam cousins and sometimes a Demers boy. Oh, and the delicious smells of your mom's baking wafting through the screen door to the kitchen when we would be playing amongst the hedge trees on your front lawn. (Almon Pope)

I especially liked the horses and cattle. I looked forward to seeing the cows in the pasture near my home when spring came and everything was a beautiful green – they looked so peaceful as they chewed their cuds. When I went into your home, I couldn't believe how many people could crowd into the kitchen – it was a very busy place. I often wondered how your mom managed to keep everyone fed, clothes washed and house cleaned. It must have been a never-ending job that required a lot of organization. I could see that all the children had their chores to do, which helped your mom and dad succeed. The Frasers always had a large garden which must have helped to cut the grocery bills – but lots of work. In the winter, I can remember taking my father's old bobsled and sliding down your hill. Often members of the Fraser family would be sliding also. We had to watch out for the traffic at the bottom of the hill and the railway crossing. Lots of fun! At times the hill would be very icy and we would end up a long ways down. I remember playing in the hayloft with you, Malcolm and Joan Cook. We would jump in the hay and slide down. One of you boys ended up with a nosebleed when someone landed on top of you. That put an end to the game for that day. Your dad used to go around checking fences and when my grandmother would spot him down in our area, she would go outside and they would have a good chat. (Dorothy Shelton Dionne)

I remember when attending Cookshire School I would be invited to the farm to celebrate my cousin June's birthday with Aunt Alice's delicious upside-down cake. Sometimes I would go down there with my parents in the evening – your parents were always busy working in the kitchen. I particularly recall from when I was very young, a planned visit that never happened. Mom had hitched up Peggy the horse to the buggy and we were all set to make the three-mile trek down to Pine Hill. However, a sudden rainstorm cancelled the trip, much to my disappointment. In recent years, I have greatly enjoyed the Fraser family reunions at the farm. (Theda Jackson Lowry)

Among the regular visitors to Pine Hill Farm were my dad's school pal, John "Pete" French (who called Dad by his childhood nickname "Honey") and his family. Pete's daughter, Muriel, recalls one particular visit:

> On a visit to the Fraser farm around 1947, when I was about six years old and my sisters Terry and Judy were 11 and 14 respectively, I remember being thrilled to actually sit on a horse. I also vividly remember your mother, Alice, nursing a baby. It was the first baby I had ever seen close up and the first time I'd ever seen anyone nursing. Alice had beautiful Irish colouring – black hair, very white skin and lovely roses in her cheeks. The whole picture was just beautiful! (Muriel French Fitzsimmons)

Visitors Muriel and Terry French with Fraser workhorse, 1947 (courtesy of Muriel French Fitzsimmons)

Our Country Garden

For more than 30 years, my wife Becky and I maintained a large vegetable garden at Pine Hill Farm. My brother Malcolm plowed and harrowed the land but we did the rest. We grew potatoes, carrots, beets, onions, string beans, corn, cucumbers, squash, zucchini and pumpkins. Normally, we did the planting on the May 24 long weekend, then travelled to the Townships every 3-4 weeks during the summer to weed the garden. Late September was harvest time: we would return home with several bushels of potatoes and carrots, plus a variable supply of onions, squash and zucchini depending on how well we maintained our plot. Naturally, we conscripted our four children to participate in this experience, about which they candidly share their memories below. Not surprisingly, they universally disliked weeding and enjoyed their break times playing by the brook! In the later years, we even enlisted the help of our first grandchild, Jacob. At the age of five, he became the seventh generation of our family to till the same land when he operated his great grandfather's hand seeder to plant the carrot seeds.

Looking back from my shady yard where almost nothing grows, my memories of gardening at Pine Hill are fond ones. I loved going up for breaks at the brook, and I liked picking carrots and beans and eating them right out of the garden! I didn't love weeding, though, especially when we used to have super-long rows. In later years we made the garden smaller and weeding didn't seem so daunting then. I liked coming home with bags and bags of produce packed all around us in the car/van. We never had to buy potatoes until way late the next spring! When our own kids were very young, they came to the farm with us as we helped with the garden. They were probably too young to remember it, but I was happy that they were able to dig around in the dirt and "help" a little. (Andrea Fraser)

The author and his grandson Jacob Fraser Lazda seeding carrots at Pine Hill Farm, ca. 2000 (photo by Andrea Fraser)

It seemed to be a very long drive to get there (with all the tolls) and an even longer drive back . . . If we did a good job weeding/working and were late arriving home, we were rewarded with Harvey's for supper! Memories from these trips to "the garden": Eating the sweetest carrots ever, right from the ground . . . praying that it would rain so that we wouldn't have to weed the string beans because they would rust if we touched them when wet . . . hauling 60-lb. jute bags of potatoes, carrots and onions . . . getting our union break to go to the brook and horse around while dodging the cow pies . . . getting my first pen knife from Uncle Ken's store during one of those trips to do gardening . . . drinking awesome water from an old ice cream tub . . . watching Mom do what seemed to be the fun jobs . . . being the horse on our makeshift manual row marker . . . waiting for the church bells to sound – meaning that we

Planting our country garden at Pine Hill Farm, ca. 1980. L-R: son Charles, daughters Andrea and Elaine, son-in-law Andreas (photo by author)

could go inside and eat lunch, especially Grammy's awesome bread and pies . . . drying out the crops on newspapers on the front lawn when we got back home . . . weeding carrots in the early stage of germination, a huge challenge and pain in the rear end . . . hauling sacks of crops to the basement for Grampa and him slipping me a $5 bill! . . . talking with Uncle Moose and touring the barns, etc. . . . picking stones, another

Marking the rows in our garden plot at Pine Hill Farm, ca. 1995. L-R: daughter Andrea, son-in-law Andreas, son Charles (photo by author)

pain-in-the-rear-end job that always seemed to be my job . . . picking off potato bugs into a margarine dish, then killing them with gasoline . . . Planting corn was what I enjoyed most – using the hoe, I didn't have to crouch down. As a kid, I can't say that gardening was fun, but now these are the types of chores that I enjoy doing on the weekend. Crazy, eh! (Charles C. Fraser)

A vivid memory is weeding the rows, in the summer heat, that seemed to go on forever. My "preference" (as weeding was not a favourite task) was weeding the potatoes or larger veggies. Carrots were so hard to differentiate between weed and plant. Your patience in showing me exactly what to pick was always appreciated. I remember that we would leave early for the trip to the farm so that we could get the weeding done before the midday heat – although I never saw you or Mom stop working. As kids, we'd be down by the creek "cooling off" when we'd

Daughter Elizabeth planting onion sets, 1987 (photo by author)

finished our rows! Hearing Grammy Fraser call from the porch "Dinner time!" was music to my ears. Ham stew and cherry pie – yum! I remember pumpkins, too, and my favourite vegetable, zucchini! They would be MEGA and to this day, I love boiled or fried zucchini with salt and pepper. The taste of garden-fresh vegetables still stays with me today. (Elaine Fraser)

As a young girl, gardening at my dad's childhood farm was a family affair rooted in hard work and an appreciation for nature. Looking back, I'm not sure just how helpful I was per se, but I was always made to feel like my contributions, as small as they may have been, were valued. I remember enjoying the harvest season the most and weeding the least. We always enjoyed picnic lunches in a shaded area in the woods next to the garden. I particularly enjoyed gazing out upon the pasture to see Grandpa's (and later Uncle Moose's) cows. I realize now just how fortunate we kids were to have the opportunity to engage in such rich, hands-on experiences connecting with nature and with those who tended the land for generations before us. (Elizabeth Fraser)

Family Feuds

Every family – especially a large one like ours – has its share of conflicts and disagreements. You know what I mean – sisterly squabbles and brotherly bickering. Obviously, we siblings didn't always see eye to eye on everything, but any differences were usually healed by the passage of time or the peacekeeping parleying of our parents. But such amicable resolutions of quarrels did not always happen in earlier generations of Frasers, as the following true stories reveal.

In 1898 my grandfather, Charles Ira Fraser and his siblings (and their families) were sued by their older brother, Jared Cook Frasier. Yes, there was an actual lawsuit that filled three pages, and the defendants were summoned to court in Sherbrooke. Jared, the plaintiff, launched the action from Colusa County in California where he had moved some years earlier. In the suit, he demanded a share of the estate of their deceased brother, William Donald, who had died without a will. Several months later, in a judgment handed down on March 30, 1899, Jared won the case. As a result, the late William's property was ordered to be

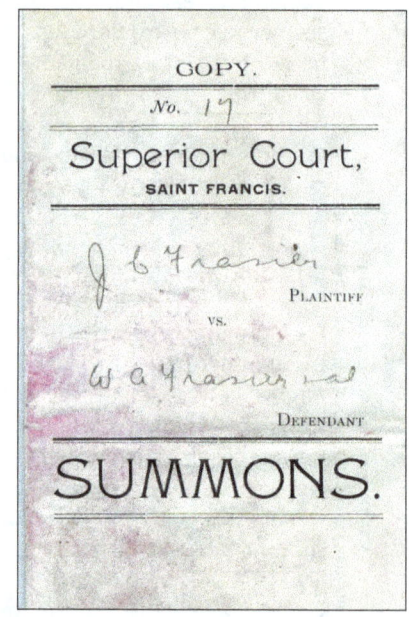

Summons re lawsuit by Jared Cook Frasier vs. his siblings, 1898 (Fraser family archives)

sold by auction and the proceeds distributed according to a complex formula proposed by Jared in his original suit. Jared's share was six eighty-fourths (6/84), as was that of each of his living siblings. Descendants of his deceased siblings were accorded lesser shares, some as little as one eighty-fourth (1/84). One has to wonder whether it was all worth it.

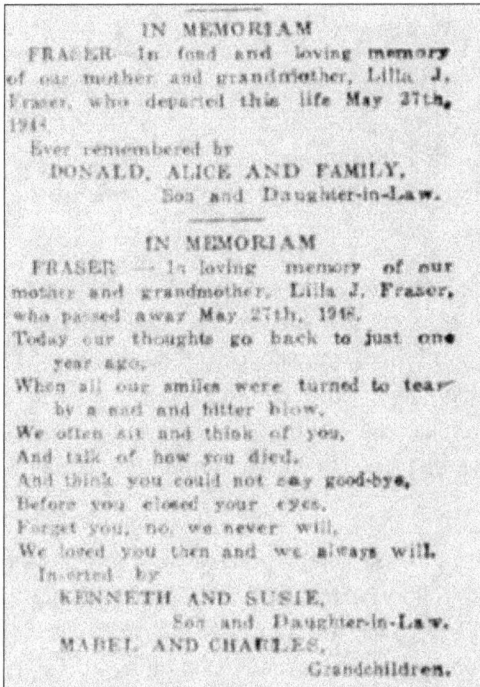

Lilla Fraser In Memoriam (*Sherbrooke Daily Record*, May 28, 1949)

Another situation that falls into the family feud framework (or perhaps more appropriately the "unsolved mysteries" category) directly involved my dad. As indicated in Chapter 5, when he purchased Pine Hill Farm from his late father's estate in 1928, he agreed to take care of his mother, Lilla, in his home for the rest of her life. He renewed the same commitment when he and my mom were married in 1933. For the following 15 years, my parents faithfully honoured that promise. When my grandmother became bedridden after a stroke, the challenges to provide for her care increased, especially for my mom who was her mother-in-law's principal caregiver. At the same time, she was very busy caring for her own growing family. In April 1948, my dad's sister, Maude, who was living in Lake Megantic at the time, offered to take Grammy into her home for a short while in order to give my mom a break. Within a month after arriving in Lake Megantic, Grammy died very suddenly, supposedly of natural causes. But my dad obviously thought otherwise. Exactly how Grammy died remains a mystery. It is interesting that an In Memoriam by her son, Kenneth, and family, published in the *Sherbrooke Daily Record* on the first anniversary of her passing contains the following lines:

> "We often sit and think of you,
> And talk of how you died."

It is also very curious that the inside cover of one of my mom's diaries from that period contains the following standalone text: "Matricide – One who murders his mother." Since one of Mom's guiding principles was to never put anything in writing that she wouldn't want others to see, I have to believe that her inscription of this random definition entry was intentional. Be that as it may, the fact remains that his mother's sudden death marked the end of my dad's relationship with his sister and her family. As far as I am aware, they never spoke again and she never again set foot in our home. Consequently, my siblings and I never got to know Aunt Maude's family. Sadly, that is how families sometimes fall apart.

Amazing Miracles

One cannot grow up on a farm without believing in miracles because miracles are everywhere. Witnessing the birth of a calf or a litter of piglets or watching the hatching of chicks or ducklings. Seeing a tiny turnip seed germinate into a huge vegetable. Savouring the miracle of the maple tree. These are just a few of the farm's everyday miracles.

Of course, when we use the word "miracle" we are more likely referring to something more dramatic, such as when a person is healed of a serious condition. Pine Hill Farm has experienced some of that type of miracle as well. As young kids, my siblings and I came down with many of those common but dangerous childhood diseases such as measles, mumps, chicken pox and whooping cough. My brother Steve had whooping cough when he was a mere infant and his survival was nothing short of a miracle.

My dad also cheated death – on at least three different occasions. The first was when he suffered a ruptured appendix while working in Shawinigan in the late 1920s. At that time, this was an extremely serious situation that often resulted in death. His second brush with death happened on the farm when a young horse he was "breaking" (i.e., training) turned on him, knocking him to the ground and trampling on his stomach. It was indeed a miracle that he was able to survive the blood loss before being taken to the hospital. The third time that death came knocking on my dad's door was in Cookshire at the blacksmith shop on Spring Street where the team of horses he was driving almost backed up over a steep drop-off. But for the just-in-time intervention of a bystander, it would have been a calamity for both man and beasts.

A very different type of miracle occurred at Pine Hill Farm in the summer of 1941.

Newborn Hereford calf, 1988 (photo by Tim Fraser)

Dad's horse attack hospitalization (sketch by James Harvey)

Fast as Lightning

They say that lightning never strikes in the same place twice. But don't you believe it for a minute. Pine Hill Farm seemed to often be the target of Thor's thunderous wrath. Every summer, the old sink room sugar camp telephone would ring by itself whenever a flash of lightning was accompanied by a simultaneous deafening "pistol-shot" thunder blast. Apart from scaring us kids out of our wits, most of these occurrences were benign. But on at least three occasions, our buildings were struck. I clearly remember two of them. When I was about five years old, a commotion downstairs and the smell of smoke awakened me in the middle of the night. Lightning had struck the side of the house, breaking a living room window and starting a fire. Fortunately, Dad was able to extinguish the flames before any further damage was done. About five years later, lightning struck the machine shed, slicing the attached clothesline pole in two.

However, the most serious lightning strike occurred in August 1941 when the lower barn was struck and set on fire. My grandmother's diary records it very matter-of-factly: "Barn struck by lightning." The details of this near-disaster are contained in the following article I wrote for an American farm magazine *The Evener* in 1985 based on my dad's recounting of the event:

> To many, "strength," "grace" and "beauty" describe the qualities of draft horses. However, my 87-year-old father, who farmed with horses for 60 years, offers yet another description: Speed. Yes, speed! It was mid-August and the haying was almost finished. The weather was hazy, hot and humid. It was the kind of day when you perspired profusely without even lifting a pitchfork. A day in which the horses' heavy harness would slip and slide in a sea of sweat. That day in August, my dad had finished haying the nearby high land and was working on the far meadow. Although the meadowland was less than a half-mile away from our farmstead, it seemed much further. To get there, we had to descend a steep gravel road, cross two railroads, ford a river and negotiate a narrow, winding trail through the riverside willow thicket. The trip from the farmstead to the meadow hay land took 10 to 15 minutes, and the trip back took longer because of the steep upgrades over most of the distance. On that memorable day, my dad was working at the far end of the quarter-mile-long field. He was tumbling the freshly-raked timothy hay into small "cocks." His cousin and frequent helper, Charlie, would soon come to help with the loading and hauling. Dad's young team of draft horses was already hitched to the wooden-wheeled hay wagon in readiness for that task. The team stood quietly nearby. Occasionally, one of them would paw the ground or nip the other's neck. As Dad finished collecting the last few scatterings of hay, he looked at the sky. Because he seldom carried a watch, it was his way of telling the time of day. And he was surprisingly accurate — usually within five or 10 minutes of the correct time. How close his estimate was that afternoon will never be known. As he leaned on his pitchfork and glanced skyward, he forgot about the time, for the sky spelled trouble.
>
> Big black thunderclouds were fast approaching. Realizing how sudden and severe summer storms can be, Dad quickly sought cover. As he hurriedly threw a few forkfuls of hay onto the wagon, a loud clap of thunder echoed through the valley. Almost immediately there was a second heavy clap, followed by a blinding flash of lightning. Just then, my

dad spotted his cousin racing across the field toward the hay wagon. Together they sought shelter under the partially loaded hayrack. As they huddled near the ground, Dad peered toward the western horizon. Above the barns, high on the hill, he saw a most unusual sight. "Hey, Charlie, look at the fog up there above the barn!" he shouted. Charlie crawled to where he could see, then exclaimed, "That's not fog, it's smoke! The barn's been struck by lightning!"

Instantly, the men leaped onto the wagon and the horses galloped at full speed across the meadow. The first quarter-mile was relatively easy — no hills, no trees and no bumps except for the occasional dead furrow. The young draft team didn't let up as they entered the willow thicket on the river bank. If anything, they went even faster. It was almost as though they, too, sensed the emergency. As they neared the most hazardous part of the route, the Eaton River, they charged down the rocky bank and plunged into the knee-deep waters. The men struggled to hold on as the wooden-wheeled wagon bounced over the slippery stones of the river bottom. As the trusty team clambered up the opposite bank, they passed the halfway point in this epic journey. But the toughest test still lay ahead of them. From here on, it was uphill all the way. Normally Dad rested the horses about every 100 feet on the steep upgrade, but they weren't rested this time.

As they emerged from the cover of the alder bushes, the barn came into view. The wind had shifted and was now blowing thick smoke toward the house. Dad began to fear the worst. With a frantic jerk of the lines, he spurred the exhausted team on. The horses responded like Olympic marathon runners who somehow find the energy to sprint the final 100 metres. They attacked the hostile hill at a punishing pace. Miraculously, no trains were blocking the crossings. (Most days they did.) As they bounded over the tracks, Charlie jumped from the wagon and ran to a neighbor's house to call the town fire department. This effort proved fruitless. Because the storm had caused a power outage, the fire whistle could not be sounded. Not a minute too soon, the horses conquered the hill, delivering my dad home.

The situation was critical. Flames were shooting from the barn roof. Dad's most immediate concern was the hay which almost filled the barn. He knew that the moment flames touched it, the barn would become an inferno. Because of the wind's direction, the fire would likely claim the farmhouse as well. Armed with pails of water from the nearby horse watering barrel, Dad and Charlie raced into the burning barn. They scrambled up the vertical ladder to the scaffold at the top of the hayloft. There they saw hungry flames feeding on the chaff which had accumulated on the upper cross-beams. The tinder-dry timothy hay lay barely a foot beneath. The first pail of water challenged the flames. The fire hissed, as if in anger. A second pail continued the fight. The fire started to sputter. Several pails later, the chaff fire was extinguished. They had won a critical battle, but the war was far from over.

The day lightning struck the barn (sketch by James Harvey)

The unattended team of draft horses watched in solemn silence as smoke and flames continued to pour from the roof. The fire was obviously eating away at the boards which lay beneath the tin. The men had to get at those flames — and fast. If even one little piece of burning debris dropped into the hay, it would be like setting a torch to a Christmas tree. Within seconds, Dad and Charlie frantically ripped large sheets of tin from the roof and poured pail after pail of water onto the stubborn flames. They soon began to gain the upper hand, and within half an hour the fire was out. The barn had been saved! As Dad turned from the barn, he cast a proud and grateful glance toward the farm gate. There stood the four-legged heroes of this victory — a pair of work horses who were almost faster than lightning! (Winston Fraser, "Meeting the Challenge at Lightning Speed," *The Evener*, 1985)

Burnt barn wall and roof from lightning strike in 1941 (photo by author)

Unsolved Mysteries

Sometimes having too much data raises more questions than answers. Such is the case of my Grandmother Fraser's 1912-1916 expense records for her children's clothes and more specifically for her teenaged son Donald's shoes. As shown in the following table, during that five-year period, she bought no less than 11 pairs of shoes for my dad (not to mention half a dozen times she paid to have them repaired). But why? There is no obvious answer. This remains a Fraser family mystery.

Amongst the trove of treasures I found in the old wooden trunk were literally hundreds of old bills and statements from local merchants with whom my ancestors traded. In spite of the weathered

Purchases of Shoes for Donald, 1912-1916

Year	Date	Cost
1912	Jan 27	$2.90
1912	Jun 26	$3.25
1913	Jul 15	$2.25
1913	Nov 7	$3.00
1914	May 16	$3.25
1914	Oct 10	$4.00
1915	May 7	$4.25
1915	Aug 27	$3.75
1916	Apr 14	$3.25
1916	Aug 11	$1.25
1916	Oct 25	$3.00

(data from Fraser family archives)

McNicol & Osgood account statement, 1875 (Fraser family archives)

condition of some of the invoices and the challenging handwriting on others, I was able to decipher most of the items, including "100 lbs. middling" (a type of second-quality flour), Kruschen salts (a laxative) and what looked like "2 bush rats" (which I believe is actually "two bushels of oats"!). However, some mysteries remain. For example, an 1875 statement from McNicol & Osgood shows that the goods purchased by my grandfather Charles were paid for by 25 lbs. of maple sugar and 25 yards of flannel. I have no idea how they would have made flannel on the farm. And in 1910, Charles settled a bill by trading 50 lbs. of "powder." What kind of powder it could have been, I do not know – another unsolved mystery.

My dad once told me about a young boy, Ronald Shorten, who worked for them on the farm for a while, then suddenly left one day in the middle of the night, never to be seen (by them) again. Also missing were my dad's few valuables, including his school medal made from Lord Nelson's battleship and some gold nuggets from his prospecting days. My Grammy Fraser, who lived with my parents, records the event in her diary entry of September 30, 1938: "Went to Megantic . . . August 17, returning home September 28 . . . While absent, Ronald S. ransacked the house, taking everything of any value . . ." In doing research for this book, I discovered two interesting references to a person of the same name. On September 12, 1938, the *Sherbrooke Daily Record* reported that 16-year-old Ronald Shorten had been missing since August 30 and that he was last reported in Cookshire at the home of Donald Fraser. Two days later, on September 14, *La Tribune* newspaper reported that the boy had been found in Ottawa. However, what happened to the family jewels remains a mystery.

POLICE SEARCH FOR VANISHED BISHOPTON BOY

16-Year-Old Ronald Shorten Has Been Missing Since August 30 — Thought Lad May Have Left Sherbrooke with Fair.

Police of Sherbrooke and communities throughout the district are conducting an intensive search for Ronald Shorten, sixteen years of age, who has been missing since August 30th.

The youth was last reported in Cookshire at the home of Donald Fraser. The Sherbrooke Fair was in operation on the day he disappeared and it is thought the youth may have obtained work with some branch of the midway and travelled to the next stand.

He is described as being five feet, six inches tall and weighing about 115 pounds. His complexion and hair are fair and his eyes are greyish blue in color, with a scar over the right eye. The youth was hatless and was wearing a blue windbreaker and blue trousers when he disappeared. He had been residing with his grandparents at Bishopton.

Report of Ronald Shorten disappearance (*Sherbrooke Daily Record*, Sep. 12, 1938)

Miscellaneous Musings

It is very obvious why the place where I grew up was called "Pine Hill Farm" but it is less obvious when this name was first used. It wasn't always known by that name. An old cover (letter envelope) from the early 1900s was addressed as follows: "Charles I. Frasier, 'Pinehurst', Cookshire, Quebec." An interesting historical side note is that my mom's childhood home, in nearby Learned Plain, was known as "The Pines." In any case, it is quite likely that it was my dad who christened the farm around 1965 when he commissioned his sign-painter brother,

Kenneth, to paint the name on a very large boulder unearthed during excavation of the ponds. Because of its location directly facing the CPR tracks, this sign has been seen by untold thousands of rail passengers on their way to or from the Maritimes.

Weathered painted rock below ponds at Pine Hill Farm, 2017 (photo by author)

One of the huge white pines that fell in a severe windstorm, 1990 (photo by author)

Abenaki translation of "great white pines" (toponymie.gouv.qc.ca)

Pine Hill Farm mailbox (photo by author)

Our Fraser family theme song, Under the Pines, written by my brother Warren and set to music by my sister June (and later adapted by my sister-in-law Carol Alette), was introduced at our Summer 1993 Family Reunion. Since that unveiling it has been sung and performed on many special occasions, sometimes accompanied by piano, bagpipes or violin.

Original music score for "Under the Pines" (by June Fraser Patterson)

Music score for "Under the Pines" (by June Fraser Patterson, adapted by Carol Alette)

Under the Pines

1. On the hot days of summer
The shaded lawn where we did dwell
And when the wind blew from the north
It was East Angus we could smell!
Under the pines, under the pines.

Chorus:
I'll meet you there, under the pines
Our lives we'll share, under the pines
We'll talk of the past and the joys that we had
And always, always, how we miss Mom and Dad.
Under the pines, under the pines.

2. The well-worn path out in the yard
Where we played at such a pace
"May I," "Tag," "Hide and Seek"
And no hiding around the base!
Under the pines, under the pines.

(Chorus)

3. Then on Sunday after Church
The kith and kin did abound
And storm clouds would start gathering
But Dad knew it would go around!
Under the pines, under the pines.

(Chorus)

Pine Hill Farm Property Valuations, 1853–2018

Year	Valuation
1853	$625
1883	$2,600
1902	$2,750
1916	$2,900
1938	$5,000
1965	$17,700
2018	$380,000

(data from Fraser family archives)

The property that Orsamus Bailey received as a free grant in December 1800 (or more precisely, that portion of the granted land that became today's Pine Hill Farm) has, over its history, experienced an enormous increase in value. This appreciation has been greatest over the past fifty years, as illustrated in the table above right.

Notes: The valuations are municipal valuations for tax purposes; they do not represent market-value assessments. The 2018 valuation does not include the meadowlands that were sold in 2013.

The Future

Because this book is focussed on the past, I will refrain from speculating on the future of Pine Hill Farm, except to state the obvious – it has an uncertain future. But regardless, one thing that is certain: Pine Hill Farm will live on in our memories forever. And not only in our memories – elements of the farm have already been reincarnated from the relics and remains of its past glory. When the great white pines fell or had to be taken down, my brother-in-law Dick Tracy salvaged the logs and had them sawn into lumber from which he created every kind of wooden object imaginable. As a result, every Fraser family home contains a piece of the pines of Pine Hill – at my former home in Rosemere, it was the kitchen cupboard doors.

Kitchen cupboard doors made from Pine Hill Farm fallen pines (photo by author)

My brother David rescued another element of the farm's historical presence. When the old machine shed collapsed from the decays of time and the weight of snow, he carefully retrieved its weathered boards and used them to build a cottage/workshop at his home in Saint-Denis-de-Brompton. Meanwhile, the rusted and rotting contents of the machine shed slowly sink into the sandy soil of its serene surroundings and the empty barn buildings suffer from years of neglect.

A Final Word

In writing this book, I have obtained much information and great inspiration from two local authors of long ago, L. S. Channell and C. S. Lebourveau. I found the opening and closing remarks of their respective historical volumes to be particularly poignant and I heartily commend their sentiments to you, dear reader.

> Few persons, reading any ordinary history, appreciate the amount of research necessary to obtain ample and accurate information on the

David Fraser's new cottage built from recycled boards of old Pine Hill Farm machine shed (photo by David Fraser)

Pine Hill Farm lower barn door comes unhinged, ca. 2010 (photo by author)

subjects treated . . . The aim has not been to write a romance, but simply to give the facts as they have been found, after months of research and study. (L. S. Channell, *History of Compton County*, 1896)

. . . My whole aim in writing this history was, 1st, that the rising generation might be able to look back and see what their forefathers had to endure, the hardships and difficulties they had to master in clearing up the forests, removing the stumps, levelling and preparing the soil, for the mower, reaper, horse rake, teader and all modern improvements, which a good share of them never lived to see, all of which we now enjoy, and should appreciate by doing our best in preparing for finer machines which will surely supersede those of to-day . . . (C. S. Lebourveau, *A History of Eaton*, 1894.)

Scrap heap of old Pine Hill Farm machinery, 2019 (photo by author)

Epilogue

Panoramic view of Pine Hill Farm from Learned Plain, ca. 1960 (photo by author)

Now I can finally relax.

My trilogy of family ancestry books is complete. It all started about 50 years ago when my dad's 92-year old cousin gave me a very weathered brown envelope stuffed with documents to be used in writing his official biography. Although I had every intention of honouring his request, it wasn't until many decades later I began putting pen to paper. Free time was in short supply in those days – what with raising a family of four children, holding down a full-time job as the family breadwinner and serving as a volunteer with several non-profit organizations.

As I slowly moved forward with Cousin Charlie's biography, a dramatic event occurred that would have an enormous impact on my writing career. My dear wife of 48 years suddenly died of a massive heart attack. In the painful process of going through Becky's belongings, I came across notes and a partial manuscript for a book that she had been intending to write about her childhood. Then and there I resolved to complete her unfinished work. So, with the help of her brother, cousins and close friends, I worked on her book in parallel with Cousin Charlie's life story. Rather than being overwhelmed with the additional workload, I felt inspired and energized, even in the midst of my grief. In fact, in retrospect, my writing served as therapy for my emotional pain. Within 12 months, both books had been published.

As it turned out, that experience opened the floodgates. In the succeeding three years, I would author two more historical volumes as well as a book featuring my photography entitled *Endangered Species of Country Life*.

Although I presently plan to take a breather, there is no guarantee how long it will last, now that I have been bitten by the writing bug.

Until next time . . .

Winston

Bibliography

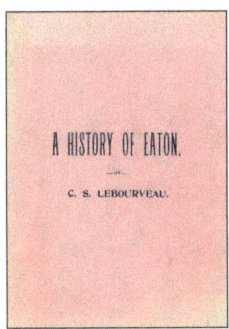

While certainly not an exhaustive listing, following are some of the published sources of information I found particularly helpful:

Books

- Channell, L. S. *History of Compton County*. Cookshire, Que.: L. S. Channell Publishing, 1896.
- Day, Catherine Matilda. *A History of the Eastern Townships*. 1869.
- Laberee, Waymer S. *The Early Days of Eaton, vol. 1*. Sherbrooke, Que.: Progressive Publications (1970) Inc., 1980.
- Lebourveau, C. S. *A History of Eaton*. 1894.
- (editor not specified). *Cookshire 1892–1992*. Cookshire, Que.: 1992.
- Neering, Rosemary and Stan Garrod. *Life of the Loyalists*. Markham, Ont.: Fitzhenry & Whiteside, 1995.

Newspapers

- *Colebrook Chronicle*, Colebrook, N.H., 2013
- *Compton County Chronicle*, Cookshire, Que., 1891-1916.
- *Journal Le Haut-Saint-François*, Cookshire, Que., 1987-2019
- *La Tribune*, Sherbrooke, Que., 1910-2019
- *Le Devoir*, Montreal, Que., 2018
- *Sherbrooke Daily Record / Sherbrooke Record / The Record*, Sherbrooke, Que., 1897-2019

Other References

- Fraser Family Link, various editions, 1991-2019
- A wide range of Internet-sourced documents

www.ingramcontent.com/pod-product-compliance
Lightning Source LLC
Chambersburg PA
CBHW070732020526
44118CB00035B/1212